The
Authorised
Kate Bane

by **Ella Hickson**

Traverse Theatre, Edinburgh, 12th – 26th October 2012
Tron Theatre, Glasgow, 30th October – 3rd November 2012

The
Authorised
Kate Bane

by **Ella Hickson**

Cast

ALBIN GOTOLD	**Nicky Elliott**
KATE BANE	**Jenny Hulse**
NESSA BANE	**Anne Kidd**
IKE BANE	**Sean Scanlan**

Creative Team

Director	**Ben Harrison**
Producer	**Judith Doherty**
Assistant Director	**Finn den Hertog**
Composer	**Michael John McCarthy**
Set and Costume Designer	**Becky Minto**
Lighting Designer	**Alberto Santos Bellido**
Production Manager	**Zoë Squair**
Technical Manager	**Robin Sanders**
Stage Manager	**Kieron Johnson**
Deputy Stage Manager	**Samantha Burt**
Video Designer	**Lewis den Hertog**
Set Build	**Big House Events**
Graphic Design	**Emma Quinn**
Finance and Development Manager	**Deborah Crewe**

Cast and Crew

Nicky Elliott (ALBIN GOTOLD)
Nicky is a stage and screen actor whose past theatre, television and film includes: *Decky Does a Bronco* (Grid Iron); *The Hard Man* (Scottish Theatre Consortium); *Kitchen*, *Lip Service*, *Life of Riley* (BBC); *Legacy*, *Salome*, *I, Keano*, *A Day in the Life*, *A Christmas Carol*, *Fair City*, to name but a few. Most recently he was seen as the devilish narrator in *The 27 Club* at this year's Edinburgh Festival Fringe. He is very privileged to be part of the Grid Iron team again and honoured to be a part of such a great cast debuting *The Authorised Kate Bane*.

Jenny Hulse (KATE BANE)
Jenny trained at the Royal Scottish Academy of Music and Drama. Previous theatre includes: *Wonderland* (Vanishing Point); *Hot Mess* (Latitude/Arcola); *Be My Baby* (Derby); *Beauty and the Beast* (Glasgow Citizens); *Sense* (Frozen Charlotte); *Every One*, *The Lion, the Witch and the Wardrobe* (Royal Lyceum); *Bright Black* (Vox Motus); *The Snow Queen*, *Cinderella* (Carnegie Hall, Dunfermline); *Hidden* (Vanishing Point/RSAMD); *The World Turned Upside Down* (Oràn Mór); *Falling* (Poorboy). Television and film includes: *The Wee Man* (Carnaby Films); *The Adventures of Daniel*, *Walter's War* (BBC); *Eadar Chluich* (BBC Alba); *Taggart* (SMG). Radio includes: *Legacy* (BBC7); *McLevy* (BBC Radio 4).

Anne Kidd (NESSA BANE)
This is Anne's first show with Grid Iron. Recent theatre includes: a site-specific play called *Manchester Lines* (Manchester Library); *The Kiss*, *Cold Turkey at Nana's* (Oràn Mór). The last time she appeared at the Traverse was in *Perfect Days*, and at the Tron in *Waltz of the Cold Wind*. Other companies she has worked with include: Dogstar, Mull Theatre, Royal Lyceum, Perth, Dundee and many shows with 7:84. Film includes: *Red Road*, *The Jacket*, *Sweetie*, *Gregory's Two Girls*. Television includes: *River City*, *Happy Holidays*, *How Not to Live Your Life*, *Still Game*, *Recovery*, *Commander Two*, *Tutti Frutti*.

Sean Scanlan (IKE BANE)

Sean trained at Drama Centre London. This is his first play with
Grid Iron. Other theatre includes: *Strangers Babies*, *The Hard
Man*, *Not Waving*, *One Day All This Will Come to Nothing*, *Widows*
(Traverse); *The Entertainer*, *Loves Lies Bleeding* (Citizens);
Brimstone and Treacle, *Says I Says He*, *The Alchemist*, *The
Changeling* (Sheffield Crucible); *Timon of Athens*, *Love for Love*,
The Glass Menagerie, *Guys and Dolls* (Bristol Old Vic); *In the
Blood*, *The Winter Dancers*, *The Weir* (Royal Court); *Hedda Gabler*
(Leicester Haymarket); *Vivat, Vivat Regina* (Mermaid); *Victoria*
(RSC); *Soft Shoe Shuffle* (Lyric Hammersmith); *The Life of Stuff*
(Donmar Warehouse). Sean has worked extensively in television,
film and radio. He has also worked numerous times at Oràn Mór.

Ella Hickson (Writer)

Ella Hickson's debut play *Eight* (Bedlam Theatre, Edinburgh) won a
Fringe First Award, the Carol Tambor 'Best of Edinburgh' Award
and was nominated for an Evening Standard Award. It transferred
to the Trafalgar Studios, London, and PS122, New York. Her other
plays include *Precious Little Talent* (Bedlam Theatre, Edinburgh
and Trafalgar Studios, London); *Hot Mess* (Hawke & Hunter,
Edinburgh and Latitude Festival); *Soup* (Òran Mór at Traverse
Theatre, Edinburgh); *PMQ* (Theatre 503 and HighTide Festival);
Boys (HighTide Festival, Nuffield Theatre, Southampton and Soho,
London) and *The Authorised Kate Bane* (Grid Iron at Traverse
Theatre, Edinburgh and Tron Theatre, Glasgow). She completed a
creative writing MA at the University of Edinburgh and spent a year
working with the Traverse Theatre as their Emerging Playwright on
Attachment. She has taken part in the Royal Court Invitation
Group and is the Pearson Playwright in Residence for the Lyric
Hammersmith. Ella is under commission to Headlong Theatre, the
Royal Shakespeare Company and Radio 4, and is participating in
Channel 4's Screenwriting Course. She is a member of the Old Vic
New Voices and has taken part in the *24 Hour Plays, Ignite* and
the T.S. Eliot UK/US Exchange. She is delighted to be working
with Grid Iron on *The Authorised Kate Bane*.

Ben Harrison (Director)

Ben is Co-Artistic Director of Grid Iron. His productions for the
company include: *The Bloody Chamber*, *Gargantua*, *Decky Does
a Bronco*, *Fermentation*, *Those Eyes*, *That Mouth*, *The Devil's
Larder*, *Roam* (with NTS); *Once Upon A Dragon*, *Yarn*, *Tryst*,

Barflies, *Huxley's Lab*, *Spring Awakening* and *What Remains*. He works extensively around the world as a freelance director, recent credits include the twenty-month US tour of *Peter Pan* for 360 Entertainment which was seen by more than a million people. Recent freelance credits in Scotland include *The Tailor of Inverness* for Dogstar, *This Twisted Tale* for the Paper Doll Militia, and *Hadda and Hassan Lekliches!* for NTS/Oràn Mór. Future projects include *Biding Time (remix)* for A Band Called Quinn, his first opera *Bolted* for Sound Festival and *Bedsheets* for Paper Doll Militia/Shams Theatre Beirut. Further information at www.benharrison.info

Judith Doherty (Producer)

Judith is the Producer, Chief Executive and Co-Artistic Director of Grid Iron. She founded the company in 1995. Since 2000 she has been a member of the Board of Directors of the Edinburgh Festival Fringe and she recently joined the board of NVA. Freelance work has included Edinburgh International Book Festival, Edinburgh International Festival, Edinburgh Fringe Society, Unique Events and BBC Scotland. In 2003, Judith received the Jack Tinker Spirit of the Fringe Award for her services to the festival.

Finn den Hertog (Assistant Director)

Finn den Hertog trained at RSAMD. Since graduating in 2007, Finn has worked regularly as an actor in theatre, television and radio and, more recently, as a director. Previous directing credits include: *The Tide* (Playwrights Studio Scotland); *The Last Dictator* (Oràn Mór); *What Do We Do Next?*, *Banyan Trees*, *An Employee's Guide to Scotland* (Atlas Company/Dundee Rep); as well as being one of two directors involved in INK: 24 Hour Plays as part of Mayfesto at the Tron last year. As an actor, Finn has worked with a range of companies including NTS, Grid Iron, The Traverse and Dundee Rep.

Michael John McCarthy (Composer)

Michael John is a Glasgow-based composer, musician and songwriter. His music work for theatre includes: *Educating Ronnie* (macrobert/Utter/HighTide); *Steel Magnolias* (Dundee Rep); *Truant* (NTS/Company of Angels); *Pause with a Smile* (The Arches/ Traverse); *99...100, Transform Dumfries* (NTS); *The Not-So-Fatal Death of Grandpa Fredo*, *Bright Black* (Vox Motus); *Birds and Other Things I Am Afraid Of* (Lynda Radley/Poorboy); *The Night*

Before Christmas (macrobert); *Dolls* (NTS/Hush Productions); *The Heights*, *The Art of Swimming*, *Soap!* (Playgroup); *The Coming World* (Making Strange).

Becky Minto (Set and Costume Designer)
This is Becky's sixth production for Grid Iron, others of which include: *Fierce*, *Tryst* and *Barflies*. She works mostly in Scotland but her work has been seen in Norway, Finland, Ireland, Italy and Sweden. She has designed a wide range of productions for main-house shows, site-specific and large outdoor spectacles, dance and aerial performances. Recent projects include: costume design for *Wonderland* (Vanishing Point); *Land of Giants* (Walk the Plank); *Tommy* (RCS); *Where On Earth* (Scottish Dance). Future projects include: costume design for *A Midsummer Night's Dream* (Royal Lyceum); and *Ignition* (NTS in the Shetland Isles).

Alberto Santos Bellido (Lighting Designer)
Alberto studied video production, multimedia and lighting design in London and Bristol, and has worked as a lighting designer, touring technician, publicity designer and video producer for theatre companies and performance artists from across the UK and further afield, winning numerous awards. Companies he's worked with include: Al Seed, Ivan Marcos, David Hughes Dance Co., Seeta Patel, Ramesh Meyyapan, Ben Faulks, Ish Toneel, Larv, HOAX productions, MIREN Theatre Co.

Zoë Squair (Production Manager)
After graduating in 1996 with a degree in Fine Art Sculpture, Zoë moved to Edinburgh and has developed a career in theatre, festivals and events. She has worked in various roles across her career with a mix of national organisations, arts organisations and touring companies including: Grid Iron, Edinburgh International Science Festival, Edinburgh Art Festival, Starcatchers, Imaginate, Dance Base, Traverse Theatre, Edinburgh International Book Festival, FST, Visible Fictions, Plutôt La Vie.

Robin Sanders (Technical Manager)
This is Robin's first time working with Grid Iron. Robin is an international freelance technical, site, venue, production manager and chief electrician. She works on indoor and outdoor projects

including most recently the 2012 Edinburgh International Book Festival. Robin has worked on rock to opera from Batignano to Wembley and beyond! She is looking forward to enjoying her time with Grid Iron.

Kieron Johnson (Stage Manager)
Kieron is a freelance stage manager based in Glasgow. He graduated from RSAMD in 2010 with a BA in Technical Production Arts specialising in Stage Management. His recent credits include: Stage Manager for the world premiere of two musicals, *Active Virgin* and *Towards the Moon*, at the 2012 Edinburgh Festival Fringe, and Props Technician for Scottish Opera's recent tour of *Tosca*. This summer saw Kieron in his seventh consecutive year working at the Edinburgh Festival Fringe, both on mid-scale musicals and dramas. Kieron has also worked with the BBC, The Arches, Matthew Bourne Productions, Visible Fictions, Criterion Theatre, London, and the Tron Theatre. For more information visit www.kieronjohnson.co.uk

Samantha Burt (Deputy Stage Manager)
Samantha Burt recently graduated from the Royal Conservatoire of Scotland with a BA in Technical and Production Arts, specialising in Stage Management. After graduating, she deputy stage-managed *Company* for One Academy productions at the Edinburgh Festival Fringe and *The Annual Showcase* for the Dance School of Scotland at the King's Theatre in Glasgow. Samantha worked as a crew member for the Traverse Theatre during the 2011 Edinburgh Festival Fringe, this led to her working in New York for the TEAM on *Mission Drift* in January 2012. As part of her Stage Management degree she has deputy stage-managed the rock opera *Tommy* in the New Athenaeum Theatre.

Deborah Crewe (Finance and Development Manager)
Deborah has worked with Grid Iron for the past nine years, although she has been closely involved with the company, as a member of the Board of Directors, since it began in 1995.

Grid Iron is an Edinburgh-based new-writing theatre company which specialises in creating site-specific and location theatre, although we also periodically produce work for the stage. Founded in 1995, we have received twenty-seven awards and a further twenty nominations covering all aspects of our work, from acting, writing, design and use of music to stage management and technical expertise.

> **'Grid Iron is not just a Scottish national treasure**
> **but one of the companies that has shaped British theatre**
> **over the last twenty years.'** Guardian

Some of the more challenging and unusual locations we have performed in include a boat-builders' island in Norway, the land-side and air-side passenger areas of Edinburgh International Airport, a former jute mill in Dundee, the former General Security building in Beirut, a working cancer hospital in Jordan, the old city morgue in Cork, Debenhams department store in Edinburgh, ten metres underwater in Belfast's Lagan Weir, a haunted underground street in Edinburgh, the London Dungeon, parks, gardens and playgrounds all over Britain and Ireland, the Medical School Anatomy Department and the Informatics Forum of the University of Edinburgh, as well as pubs and theatre bars all over Scotland and beyond.

Our growing international reputation has brought us two European Capital of Culture commissions, for Cork 2005 and Stavanger 2008, and an extensive programme of work for the British Council in the Middle East. We have also produced with National Theatre of Scotland, the Traverse Theatre, Edinburgh, the Almeida Theatre, London, Edinburgh International Festival, the Burns an' a' That! Festival, Lung Ha's Theatre Company and Dundee Rep Theatre, as well as performing as part of Cork's Fringe (now Midsummer) Festival and the Belfast Festival at Queens.

> **'Grid Iron, one of Scotland's boldest and most influential groups**
> **of the last two decades.'** Telegraph

www.gridiron.org.uk   @gridirontheatre

THE AUTHORISED KATE BANE

Ella Hickson

For M, D and T

'The unfolding drama of life is revealed more by the telling than by the actual events told. Stories are not merely "chronicles" like a secretary's minutes of a meeting, written to report exactly what transpires and at what time. Stories are less about facts and more about meanings. In the subjective and embellished telling of the past, the past is constructed, history is made.'

D.P. McAdams

'Most of us are not easily willing to part with the assumption that there is a shared external reality that is at least partly knowable through memory…That assumption is fundamental to many of society's institutions, such as our legal and education systems, and it also underlies our trust in autobiographical memory as a basis for self-understanding.'

Daniel L. Schacter

Author's Note

The genesis of *The Authorised Kate Bane* came from an increasing preoccupation I have had with authenticity in theatre as concerns form and performance. I'm sure this is very common in playwrights. The delight and relief of simply finishing plays and/or getting them produced, quickly gives way to a critical engagement with the work – 'What's it for?' 'When is it good?' and most importantly 'What is true?' When the occasions arose to discuss these questions with other practitioners, a part of my job that I most love and feel privileged to engage in, it became very clear that what I had deemed to be personal concerns were in fact political questions.

At the same time I was talking to a neuroscientist called Demis Hassabis who was doing fascinating work into how unreliable memory was. The idea that we 'wrote' our pasts more than remembered them brought the concept of character right into the centre of the question of theatrical authenticity. If characters aren't formed from their pasts, then what are they? And by extension, stories cease to be just fictions but in fact the only means we have to create any sense of 'self'. This rather disorganised collection of ideas was enough for Grid Iron to express interest. I was delighted by the idea of returning to Scotland and working on this material with a company that had formal experimentation at their heart and whom I trusted enough to take risks with.

Acknowledgements

I would like to thank Ben, Jude and Deb for the opportunity to work with a company I respect and admirė and in an environment that facilitates experiment and excellence; I am deeply grateful. I would like to thank Demis Hassabis for being so generous with his time and knowledge. My thanks to the cast and crew for their time, talent and ideas; my thanks too to David Greig for his continued advice – I am a braver writer because of it. My continued thanks go to Jess Cooper. Last – but by no means least – my thanks to my family and my boyfriend for their unflinching support and understanding.

E.H.
London, 2012

Characters

KATE BANE, *thirty*
IKE BANE, *sixty-two*
ALBIN GOTOLD, *thirty-four*
NESSA BANE, *sixty-one*

Note on the Text

KELSO
*Dialogue/action of the 'play'. This material is the product of
Kate's imagination, she writes this material during the
performance. This dialogue/action is set in the imagined Bane
house in Kelso, Scotland.*

LONDON
*Dialogue/action set in the London flat in which Kate writes the
'play'.*

MEMORY
*Dialogue/action that is Kate's memory, these are recalled whilst
she is in her London flat, as she writes.*

EDIT
*Action/dialogue that represents rewriting or editing of the 'play'
as it is being written in London.*

A forward slash (/) in the text indicates interrupted speech.

*This text went to press before the end of rehearsals and so may
differ slightly from the play as performed.*

One

LONDON

KATE *enters her bedroom. She is dressed from an evening out. She walks into the bedroom, closes the door behind her and leans against it.*

ALBIN (*from downstairs – barely audible*). How was it?

> KATE *ignores the question.* KATE *gets changed into her pyjamas. She walks a circle around her room; she's deep in thought, frustrated.* KATE *lies on the floor, she pushes her limbs out to make a starfish shape.*

> ALBIN *knocks on the door quietly.*

(*Through the door.*) How did it go?

KATE. I'll be down in a second, just give me a second – I'll come down.

> *No response.*

ALBIN (*through the door*). How did it go?

> *Beat.*

KATE. I left.

ALBIN. Before the end?

KATE. There was no point in staying.

ALBIN. That seems a bit defeatist. (*Beat.*) Can I come in?

KATE. I'll come down. I'll come down and – I'll /

ALBIN. / Okay. Your mum rang.

KATE. Did you speak to her?

ALBIN. I introduced myself.

KATE. And?

ALBIN. And?

KATE. And?

ALBIN. She just asked if they should bring anything tomorrow.

KATE. What did you say?

ALBIN. Maybe wine.

KATE. Oh.

ALBIN. That okay?

KATE. Course. (*Beat.*) I'll come down and – do supper in a tick.

ALBIN. Okay.

KATE. Okay.

> ALBIN *leaves the other side of the door.*
>
> KATE *is left alone in the room.*
>
> KATE*'s head won't keep quiet.*
>
> KATE *walks, with some purpose – towards her computer, she is going to write – she has to write, to get it down.*
>
> *As she walks, her pyjamas come off and a smart outfit comes on.*
>
> *The sound of her footsteps shifts from slippers on a bedroom floor to feet on gravel.*

KELSO

A country cottage in Kelso, Scotland. It hasn't changed in twenty years. Family photos, souvenirs, certificates are still about the place – but the house has been perfectly maintained. It is spotless, comfortable, homely. The house is some distance from the closest train station and there is nothing but fields in walking distance. It is mid-January, the weather is bitter – it snows – and snows.

Evening, pitch black outside – the snow has been falling hard for several hours.

Inside, soft lamplight, an open fire. Three champagne glasses are set out on a tray.

IKE *arranges and rearranges a plate of canapés.*

IKE *moves several objects around on the coffee table – he stands back, looks – readjusts them for aesthetic ease, and moves away.*

IKE *pours himself a glass of champagne, knocks it back – dries the glass and places it back on the side.*

IKE *stands still. The silence of the house is palpable. A long time passes.*

A car can be heard coming down the drive – the headlights swing in through the windows.

IKE *checks things once more and then waits – by the door.*

We can hear the slamming of car doors – footsteps on gravel, on snow – the doorbell rings.

IKE *stares at the door.*

The front doorbell rings.

Pause.

The front doorbell rings.

IKE *opens the front door to* KATE *and* ALBIN. IKE *is talking on the telephone. He apologises profusely in mime, rolls his eyes – suggests the person is yapping. He mimes a 'Lovely to meet you – come in' – to* ALBIN, *who nods.*

KATE. Hi, Dad.

IKE. If they need me there then they should have rung earlier, I just can't do it – I don't care how urgent it is, Roy – I said that this weekend was out and I mean it – emergency or no emergency –

KATE. Hi.

KATE *stares at* IKE.

IKE. I'm sorry, Roy – I'm really going to have to go – I'm really going – my daughter's here – with her boyfriend and I'm –

ALBIN. It's fine.

IKE. Okay – okay – bye now.

> IKE *puts the phone back in the cradle.*

KATE. Hi, Dad.

IKE. Hello, darling.

> IKE *goes to hug* KATE. KATE *steps away, taking her jacket off and avoiding the embrace.*

> It's so wonderful to see you (*Clears her fringe from her face.*) You look – lovely.

> KATE *kisses her father on the cheek.*

KATE. Nice to see you too.

IKE. And this must be –

ALBIN. Albin, it's great to meet you. Really great – after all this time. We brought wine.

IKE. It's a pleasure.

> ALBIN *shakes* IKE*'s hand robustly.*

> ALBIN *pulls* IKE *in for a hug –* IKE *is slightly taken aback.*

ALBIN. You have a lovely home. It's so cosy.

IKE. Oh God, it's filthy; tatty. I haven't had a chance to /

KATE. / It looks lovely, Dad. Great, good.

> ALBIN *offers* IKE *a bottle of red wine.*

> IKE *puts it down on the side – starts taking their coats and hanging them up.*

IKE. Thank you. You must be freezing – let me take your coats – was the drive very long? Is it snowing? Isn't it snowing? I heard on the news that there's been more snow today than there's ever been. Who would like a drink?

KATE. What?

IKE. Snow.

KATE. More than there's ever been?

IKE. On the news.

KATE. What?

IKE. Who would like champagne? It's pink.

ALBIN. Yes please. Champagne, Kate? We've got some – Kate, we brought some –

KATE. Oh – chocolates.

IKE. How sweet, you didn't have to –

KATE. They're gingers.

IKE. My favourite, you remembered my favourite.

KATE. You love gingers.

IKE. I love gingers.

> KATE *takes the champagne.*

KATE. Thanks.

IKE. It's just the cheap stuff.

KATE. It's Moët.

IKE. It was on offer – ten for fifteen pounds.

ALBIN. Blimey – that is cheap.

IKE. Or for six or something. Come on – top you up, it's all froth. Kate?

KATE. Thank you.

IKE. I'm afraid dinner is all a bit of a mess; I just threw something together with what we had in the fridge – all a bit last-minute. Have an olive.

ALBIN. You didn't tell him we were coming?

KATE. We've had this arranged for two months.

IKE. Sit down – don't stand – come on.

ALBIN. I'm sure it will be lovely – I'm starving so anything will /

KATE. / What are we having?

IKE. Partridge with braised cabbage and dauphinois potatoes. Albin, can I offer you a parmesan puff?

IKE holds the bowl up to ALBIN.

ALBIN. Uh – yes – thank you.

KATE. Who was on the phone?

IKE. Hm?

KATE. On the phone – when we came in – it sounded like there was some kind of emergency.

IKE. Come on, sit down – we're standing around like we're at a concert or something – Kate, will you put some music on, something soothing – choral – Handel's in there, I think.

ALBIN. Poor guy.

IKE. What?

ALBIN. Stuck in the –

IKE. Aren't you tall?

ALBIN. Yes.

IKE. Are your parents tall?

Tiny beat – KATE cuts in.

KATE. Who was on the phone?

IKE. The university.

KATE. What was the drama?

IKE. Drama? Albin is Scandinavian, isn't it? Kate said you were /

ALBIN. / My father's family were Danish.

IKE. Are you very calm and collected – very cool? Very chilled out?

ALBIN. Um – I try to be, but – I don't know, am I calm and collected?

KATE. Pretty calm.

IKE. But you live in London – you've always lived in London?

ALBIN. Mostly, yeah.

IKE. Very cool – trendy – I've got friends in London. Can I get you any more?

ALBIN. I'm okay, thank you. I'm fine. It's lovely.

KATE. It sounded like there was a drama –

IKE. Oh, they wanted me to go in and cover last-minute – look over some – it's been a mess there for weeks, I'm exhausted – I've barely stopped, I can't tell you how hard this term has been.

KATE. On a Friday night?

ALBIN. Kate – parmesan puff?

KATE. Thank you. On a Friday night?

IKE. Exhausting.

ALBIN. Kate?

KATE. It just seems unlikely.

IKE. I'll get you a coaster.

ALBIN. The house is beautiful. I love these paintings, are they Scottish?

IKE. Polish. We bought them in Kraków – when we went to see the salt mines, from a stall, a little provincial stall; Kate – do you – do you remember?

KATE. No.

IKE. You don't remember Kraków?

KATE. The pictures.

IKE. You don't remember the salt mines?

KATE. Yes – I just don't remember the pictures.

IKE. But they're there – look at them.

KATE. I remember what they look like – now – yes, but I don't
remember buying them.

Beat.

IKE. It was lovely that holiday – we had such a lovely time,
didn't we have a lovely time? In the markets, all lamplit and
that funny rustic restaurant – I bought a pair of earrings for
your mother. I don't think she ever wore them. I remember
her describing them as tatty to a friend.

KATE. Did she?

IKE. She never wore them.

KATE. But I can't imagine she –

IKE. On the phone – I heard her. It hurt.

KATE. Al – parmesan puff?

IKE. Don't talk over me.

KATE. I wasn't.

IKE. It hurt.

KATE. You said.

Beat.

ALBIN. This is delicious.

IKE. It's just the cheap stuff. Kate?

KATE. Thank you.

IKE *offers* KATE *cassis for her champagne.*

IKE. Kir?

KATE. A little.

IKE. So – Albin – tell us, what is it you do? It's something
sciencey – isn't it? It's to do with – Kate – said, I'm sure.

KATE. Albin's a neuropsychologist.

ALBIN. You teach, don't you?

IKE. For my sins.

ALBIN. Creative writing?

IKE. Did you give him my inside-leg measurement?

KATE. It's your job.

ALBIN. Anyone I'd know?

IKE. Hm?

ALBIN. Have you taught any superstars?

IKE. No. (*Beat.*) Have the reviews come out yet?

KATE. No.

ALBIN. It's press night tonight /

KATE. / Al.

IKE. No. Kate?

KATE (*shoots* ALBIN *a prohibitive glare*). Not yet. No reviews.

IKE. Don't you need to be there? Don't you need to /

KATE. / You said there was one called Jade.

IKE. What?

KATE. A kid in your class that you were really excited about, she was called Jade.

IKE. Yes… she's quite amazing.

ALBIN. What's so amazing?

IKE. She's so – she's – brilliant, really.

ALBIN. Why?

IKE. She turns up late – half-cut – she's Jayde with a 'Y' – which is – anyway – she's from London somewhere, roughish, you know – (*Charmed.*) works late in a bar, gobby – says what she thinks. Earrings all over, tracksuits – I mean real attitude. But, my God, she tells the most amazing stories – wild things, ten to a bedroom, family like rogues – fights and crime and jokes and so outrageous you'd think you'd had trouble believing it but somehow it – somehow you sort of know, it's true and the language – the most amazing language – stuff you've never heard, slang and colloquialisms and the colour of it, and I can't tell you – how effortlessly – real, it is, how – authentic. This gold, this real honest gold just sings right out of the middle of her.

And the rest of the class – starts getting a little – not envious – but, you know, and they start packing their stuff to the gunnels with abortion and kiddie-fiddling and drugs and whatnot… but it just sounds so flimsy. And you feel sorry for the rest of them, all these keen students with their impressive vocabularies and all that ambition and education but they'll never write what Jayde writes because they're not… they never have anything really interesting to say for themselves.

LONDON

KATE *stops writing, she stands up from her chair. She walks slowly about the room.*

KATE *returns to the chair, tries to sit, can't.*

KATE *lights a cigarette – stares at the screen.*

KATE *begins to write and rewrite.*

EDIT

IKE. Never have anything really interesting to say for yourself.

KATE *deletes the sentence.*

KATE *rewrites the sentence.*

IKE. Never have anything fucking interesting to say for your boring little comfortable educated self.

IKE. Never never never never.

KATE *deletes the sentences.*

LONDON

KATE *goes to walk away from the computer.*

KELSO

Beat.

ALBIN. That seems a bit – defeatist.

LONDON

KATE *stops*.

KELSO

IKE. It's the case.

KATE. Can we not talk about work, please – can we leave it, it doesn't matter.

ALBIN. Do you write – I mean – yourself?

KATE. Let's just get on with – just get on –

IKE. Dinner will be a little while yet.

ALBIN. I'm really interested.

IKE. No – not really – no. I used to – but no, not now, not since... well, teaching takes up a lot of time and I've rather lost my /

KATE. / Poems – sometimes; they're good.

IKE. They're awful.

KATE. They're good.

IKE. Not as good as – (*Indicates* KATE.) obviously. I'm a pretender to her throne.

KATE. That's not true.

IKE. Of course it is. *Tramlines* is brilliant, Kate, the reviews are going to be /

ALBIN. She won't let me see it.

IKE. I've read it – it's brilliant, it's so funny and –

KATE. That cardigan's lovely, Dad.

IKE. That scene with the ballboy and the banker /

KATE. / Parmesan puff?

ALBIN. I'm fine, thank you.

IKE. There are brie-and-cranberry parcels in the oven; I'm just waiting for them to get gooey.

ALBIN. Great.

Long pause.

A beeper goes off in the kitchen.

IKE. That'll be the brie-and-cranberry. Kate, will you get the napkins out of the sideboard?

IKE exits.

KATE. I'm sorry.

ALBIN. What for?

KATE. He's…

ALBIN. He's fine. He's nice.

KATE. Yeah?

ALBIN. Yeah.

ALBIN starts walking around the room – snooping a little.

KATE watches him.

ALBIN finds a picture of NESSA on IKE's desk.

This your mum?

KATE. Yes.

ALBIN. Not how I imagined – at all. She's sort of –

KATE. Handsome.

ALBIN. Scary. She looks a bit like Stalin.

KATE. Al – that's my mum!

ALBIN. I'm joking – sort of. He's still got a picture of her on his desk. That's a bit –

KATE. I know.

ALBIN. But I thought they broke up –

KATE. Twenty years ago.

ALBIN. That seems… it's nice – to still have a picture of her.

KATE. Is it?

Pause.

He's so… I'm sorry.

ALBIN. Stop apologising.

KATE. I just don't want you to think –

ALBIN. I don't think anything.

KATE. He's just a bit /

ALBIN. / Kate, he's your dad.

KATE. I know but –

ALBIN. What?

KATE. He's difficult.

ALBIN. Is he?

KATE. I find him really hard to be around.

MEMORY

IKE *stands and looks at* KATE.

IKE *crumples, sobbing – he reaches out for* KATE *to help him.*

KATE *backs away.*

IKE. Kate? Come here?

KELSO

ALBIN. But that's not him, that's you.

KATE. Oh.

MEMORY

IKE *stands and looks at* KATE.

IKE *crumples with laughter, guffawing – he reaches out for* KATE *to help him.*

KATE *backs away.*

IKE. Kate? Come here?

KELSO

ALBIN. I didn't mean that to sound – I'm sorry I –

KATE. It's – okay.

ALBIN. I just mean – he's your dad.

LONDON

KATE *stops writing a moment – and stares at the computer screen.*

KATE *looks at* ALBIN.

KATE. Don't say it like that.

KELSO

ALBIN. He's your dad.

KATE. Don't say it like that – I love him.

ALBIN. I know.

LONDON

KATE *picks up a box of Final Draft software – looks at it.*

KELSO

ALBIN *takes the box out of* KATE*'s hand and starts reading it.*

ALBIN. It seems funny to teach this stuff if you've never done it... Listen to this: 'On Creating Character is brought to you by Final Draft, Inc. What kind of childhood would you say your character had? Happy? Or sad? What was her relationship like with her parents? Was she loved? Was she kind or spiteful? Was she ungrateful? Do you think she made friends easily, and got along well with relatives and other children? Was she difficult, selfish, manipulative? Was she kind, tolerant and loving? Was she good or bad? What kind of a child would you say she was? Was she outgoing and extroverted or shy and studious, an introvert? Let your imagination guide you.' Kate? Which one were you? Come on?

MEMORY

IKE *stands and looks at* KATE.

IKE *crumples, sobbing – he reaches out for* KATE *to help him.*

KATE *backs away – unsure.*

IKE. Kate? Come here?

IKE *stands and looks at* KATE.

IKE *crumples with laughter, guffawing – he reaches out for* KATE *to help him.*

KATE *backs away – unsure.*

IKE. Kate? Come here?

IKE *stands and looks at* KATE.

IKE *crumples, sobbing – he reaches out for* KATE *to help him.*

KATE *backs away – unsure.*

IKE. Kate? Come here?

KELSO

ALBIN (*continuing*). Hey – come here –

KATE. I don't know.

> IKE *reaches out to* KATE *with a tray of brie-and-cranberry parcels.*

IKE. Come here.

KATE. I don't know.

ALBIN. Kate?

IKE. Come here and give your dad a hug.

> KATE *backs away.*

KATE. We're not staying, Dad.

IKE. What?

KATE. We've got a room booked back up at the hotel – I told you, we spoke about that, I told you.

IKE. I made up the bed – your bedroom.

KATE. We agreed.

IKE. It's snowing. You're tired. Have a drink.

KATE. I said, I explained about needing to be back in Edinburgh by tomorrow. Al needs to be back in Edinburgh by tomorrow.

ALBIN. Not until the afternoon – really.

IKE. It's dangerous, the weather.

KATE. But, Dad – we agreed that we'd give you the space to –

IKE. Space? I don't need space – I've got nothing but space. (*Beat.*) It's snowing pretty heavily.

KATE. 'The most there's ever been'?

IKE. Really?

ALBIN. We can stay – it will be nice to stay. It means we can both have a drink and relax, it'll be nice. If you're sure there's room. We can drive back tomorrow.

KATE. We've booked the hotel.

ALBIN. We'll save money.

KATE. There'll be a cancellation charge.

ALBIN. But overall we'll save money.

IKE. I'll reimburse you.

KATE. No, that's not what I was –

I'm just saying that we need to be gone by tomorrow.

IKE. I made up the bed. I got food in for the weekend.

KATE. But we never said we would /

ALBIN. / Kate?

KATE. We can't afford to get stuck, that's all.

IKE. Stuck – you make it sound like a /

ALBIN. / We won't get stuck. It would be nice to have a bit more time together.

IKE. He's right – you're never home, make the most of it.

ALBIN. It's family – isn't it. Kate?

KATE. Yes.

LONDON

KATE *steps outside of the scene and watches the two men talking to each other.*

KELSO

IKE. It's so lovely to have you here, to have the house full – it feels like home again.

ALBIN. Just relax.

IKE. Yes. Relax. Brie and cranberry?

ALBIN. Don't mind if I do.

> *Beat.*

> Hey, look! This is you naked! I'd know that…

LONDON

KATE *takes the photo off* ALBIN *and puts it back down.*

KELSO

ALBIN. Foot. Those feet, anywhere – those toes, phff – like claws.

IKE. My fault entirely – should have seen my mother, talons.

ALBIN. You look like each other, you know. I couldn't see it in photos – but something – looking at you. It's around the eyes, I think.

IKE. Everyone always said Kate looked like her mother.

ALBIN. No – you can see it, you really can.

IKE. Albin, tell me about your parents? Do you spend a lot of time with them? Visit often?

ALBIN. No. They're – dead.

LONDON

KATE *moves past the area where the window is.*

KELSO

IKE. Oh. (*Spots something outside the window.*) Fuck.

ALBIN. It's no problem, I don't remember it. I was tiny, a car accident – I was brought up by my /

IKE. I just saw something in the window.

> ALBIN *spins around.*

ALBIN. What do you mean?

IKE. A thing – in the window – past the window – it had fur, it was huge and it had fur.

ALBIN. What?

IKE. It looked like a – bear.

ALBIN. A bear? A bear? There's a fucking bear?

LONDON

KATE *opens the door.*

KELSO

NESSA *enters with a crash, throwing the door open, and with a large 'hulloo' – a little like a roar.* ALBIN *flings himself to the floor.* NESSA *stands in the sitting room,* IKE *stares dumbstruck. She has an accordion strung across her back, huge fur-seal boots and a large fur coat on, smoking a cigar.*

NESSA. Hullo, Ikey – haven't you got old.

   KATE *enters from the kitchen.*

KATE. Mum?

NESSA. Dahling.

   NESSA *embraces* KATE.

KATE. How did you – ?

NESSA. Couple of band mates dropped me off at the end of the road, had to tramp right across the fields, I can't tell you what a –

   ALBIN *resurrects himself from his defensive position and straightens up.* NESSA *looks him up and down.*

   – damp crotch I've got.

KATE. Mum, this is Albin, my boyfriend.

ALBIN. It's a pleasure.

NESSA. No – no, all mine.

ALBIN goes in to kiss NESSA hello.

NESSA offers him her hand instead.

Keen.

IKE. Nessa.

NESSA. You can have a kiss, you I know rather well.

NESSA goes to kiss IKE hello – IKE steps back.

IKE. I've only catered for three.

NESSA. Cheer up, frosty.

IKE. What are you doing here?

NESSA. I thought I'd pop home.

IKE. Home?

NESSA. Yes, this is my house – technically – I mean, I own it. I'm Ike's landlady, Albin, you see. I'm very generous and benevolent though, I hardly interfere at all.

IKE. Landlady, yes – landed – she landed right in it, great big piles, acres and acres.

NESSA. There's no need to bring up my piles in front of Kate's new boyfriend, Ike, it's not very polite.

ALBIN. Parmesan puff?

NESSA. Thanks. Besides, I wanted to see how the old ruin was holding up.

IKE. I won't take that personally.

NESSA. Is there any chance of a drink?

IKE. No.

KATE. Yes.

NESSA. Would you pop my coat under the stairs for me?

KATE slides her mother's coat off for her.

IKE. You're not staying.

KATE *puts the coat away.*

NESSA. It's awful cold out there. (*Pointing to* ALBIN*'s drink.*) Couldn't get me one of those, Al – could you?

ALBIN *starts pouring her a drink.*

KATE. Sit down; tell us where you've been.

NESSA. In the town hall – I was calling a ceilidh. Fell in with a fiddly lot.

KATE. I thought you were in Mongolia –

NESSA. Azerbaijan – a farm.

KATE. You sent me that photo of that man with no teeth.

ALBIN *hands* NESSA *the drink.*

NESSA. Aren't you delightful?

ALBIN. Yes – um – no – am I – I mean –

NESSA *beams up at him.*

– um – am I?

KATE. Mum?

NESSA. Hm?

KATE. The man with no teeth – I thought you weren't coming back until the spring.

NESSA. Ah, Karim – still no teeth, makes up for it elsewhere. What are we eating? (*Smells the air.*) Oh, Ike, you didn't?

KATE. Braised red cabbage and dauphinois.

NESSA. Oh, Ikey – you bloody rascal – you've only gone and made my bloody favourite.

IKE. I catered for three.

KATE. We've enough for four – we'll make enough. It's family, isn't it, Al?

ALBIN. Guess so.

IKE. I catered for three.

NESSA. Stutter, darling?

IKE. We've not got enough.

NESSA (*putting her arm around* KATE). FHB.

ALBIN. FHB?

NESSA. Family Hold Back; I'm sure there's enough wine that we won't even notice.

IKE. I'll need to lay another place at the table.

NESSA. Won't take a jiffy. Families that eat together, stay together. That's what you used to say, Ike; wasn't it?

IKE. Yes.

NESSA. Well, there we go then. Let's eat!

> NESSA *puts her arm through* ALBIN's *and leads him through to the kitchen.*

> Now, Albin – tell me everything about you, I want all the gory details.

> NESSA *and* ALBIN *exit.*

> IKE *stands rooted to the spot.*

KATE. Dad?

IKE. Hm.

KATE. Let's eat.

> IKE *goes to walk past* KATE – KATE *watches him.*

MEMORY

Music starts – a waltz.

IKE *dances with an invisible ten-year-old* KATE.

IKE *laughs heartily.*

IKE *is forty-two.*

IKE. Lady Kate, your footwork is perfection. You must have been taught by a wise man – perhaps it was your father, I hope you thanked him for his efforts! You paid him in crumpets! Crumpets? The finest of payments! And your mother? A crumpet-eater too! I don't believe such a fine family exits! We should have your mother come and dance with us! (*Calling up the stairs.*) Fine woman – come and dance! Come and dance and have a crumpet! Fine woman! (*Stops dancing and looks at the doorway… softer now, less hopeful.*) Fine woman? Fine woman?

LONDON

KATE. Mum?

MEMORY

Pause.

NESSA *does not arrive.*

IKE, *downcast, walks past* KATE *and exits the room.*

LONDON

KATE *watches* IKE *go.*

KELSO

IKE *exits the sitting room.*

KATE *stands alone.*

Beat.

NESSA *pops her head in.*

NESSA. It's on the table.

KATE. Coming.

Two

KELSO

The sitting room.

Late in the evening – after dinner.

An array of discarded coffee cups and wine glasses lie around.

ALBIN *is up and being demonstrative – having had a few.*

NESSA *is actively fascinated.*

ALBIN. Okay – well, we'll do a little test.

NESSA. Oooh – yes! A test.

IKE. Do we need pen and paper?

ALBIN. No – no. It's all verbal.

IKE. Righto.

ALBIN. Ready?

NESSA. Yes, captain!

ALBIN (*to* KATE). I know you've done this before, try not to look so bored.

KATE. I'm not looking bored, I'm looking adoring. They're similar faces.

ALBIN. Lucky me. Right – I'm going to tell you a list of words –

NESSA. Do we write them down?

IKE. Let the man speak.

ALBIN. No. You have to try and remember them. Okay? Ready?

IKE. Just remember them, nothing more.

ALBIN. Yes – that's it. I'll say the whole list twice.

KATE. He is trained, Dad, just do what he says.

ALBIN. Candy, sour, sugar, bitter, taste, tooth, nice, honey, soda, chocolate –

NESSA. Yum.

ALBIN. – heart –

NESSA. Urgh.

KATE. Try not to talk, Mum.

IKE. You'll be lucky.

ALBIN. Kate – shh. Cake, eat and pie.

KATE. Me?

IKE. It was Nessa that /

NESSA. / Telltale.

ALBIN. And again – candy, sour, sugar, bitter, taste, tooth, nice, honey, soda, chocolate, heart, cake, eat and pie.

NESSA. Got them.

IKE *is working very hard to remember.*

Look at the concentration on him.

ALBIN. Right – now tell me – was the word 'point' on the list?

IKE. No.

NESSA. No.

ALBIN. Correct.

NESSA. Even stevens, Ikey.

ALBIN. Was 'taste' on the list?

NESSA. Yes.

IKE (*more hesitant*). Yes – yes, it was.

ALBIN. Correct.

They both celebrate in their own small way.

Was 'sweet' on the list?

NESSA. Yes.

IKE. N – yes – yes. No – yes. Yes.

ALBIN. All bets in?

IKE. Yes.

ALBIN. Incorrect.

IKE. What?

ALBIN. Not there.

IKE. 'Sweet' was definitely on the list.

ALBIN. It wasn't there, I promise.

NESSA. Hm, strange.

IKE. It was definitely on the list.

KATE. It wasn't, Dad.

ALBIN. Your brain thinks it was because the list had so many words on it that associated with 'sweet'.

IKE. Bullshit.

ALBIN. Um – no – the conditions of the question cause you to think. /

IKE. / I heard 'sweet'.

ALBIN. It wasn't there.

IKE. Are you saying I'm wrong?

NESSA. He's not saying you're wrong – you are wrong.

ALBIN. You imagined a memory.

IKE. I'm not sure I follow.

NESSA. Well, you're certainly not leading, dear.

ALBIN. The environment in which you recall a memory influences the content of that memory as much as – if not more than – the actual event that you are remembering. Now is – more important than then – in terms of /

IKE. / But I remember things… clearly.

ALBIN. They may be clear but they aren't accurate depictions of what actually happened.

IKE. I feel them /

NESSA. / I'm sure you do.

ALBIN. / But that isn't – any more of a – it's just a neurological process – the engram is valid, it's just its relation to the actual event is unreliable.

IKE *bows out.*

NESSA. Isn't that attractive?

IKE *stands up and starts to clear the glasses.*

ALBIN. Yes, it completely revolutionises the way we think about the past and the formation of the idea of self and /

NESSA. / No – you talking like that, those words – it's very attractive, isn't it, Kate?

KATE. Um – Dad, no – don't do that, you did dinner /

IKE (*snaps*). *Do* shut up, Nessa!

Beat.

ALBIN. I'll clear up.

IKE. It's fine.

NESSA. Oh, look at the bloody museum-keeper having a sulk; 'I don't like being told I'm wrong – woof woof woof.'

IKE. I'm fine, thank you.

NESSA. You see, Albin – Ike is somewhat of an archivist, a recorder – (*Pretends to play the recorder.*) He finds the flimflam of subjectivity rather destabilising, would rather have a nice tidy account of things to rely on; stops him feeling queasy. Rules and regulations – right and wrong – jot it down and make it stick – that's how you like it, isn't it?

KATE. Mum – leave him alone.

IKE. I'm fine, thank you.

NESSA. Compulsive scribbler – never happy until he's got it on paper, you'd be playing at something – having a laugh and then there'd be this funny little silence and a scratchy scribble – I can't tell you how depressing the appearance of a post-coital notepad is. Can't help but feel scrutinised. More wine, anyone?

IKE. I've had enough.

KATE *and* ALBIN *signal no.*

NESSA. Suit yourselves. (*Pours herself another glass.*) Kate, do you remember being on safari and we saw the most amazing flock of flamingos?

KATE (*smiling*). Yes – yes – I really do, that's so weird, yeah – it was incredible.

NESSA. Al, we saw this incredible flock of flamingos and Ike –

IKE. A stand.

NESSA. What?

IKE. A stand of flamingos.

NESSA. But they weren't standing, they were flying – that's the whole point.

KATE. It's still a stand of flamingos.

NESSA. Anyway, this bunch of flamingos flew overhead – and Ike leapt to his pen and paper, ready to scribble and by the time he looked up they'd gone. It was very funny at the time. Him looking up all – 'bugger it' – and seeing nothing but a jet stream of flamingo fart. But in retrospect, it's a little sad.

IKE. That didn't happen.

NESSA. Yes it did.

IKE. I saw them, I watched them.

NESSA. Kate – he did, didn't he?

KATE. I just remember the flamingos.

NESSA. Scribble scribble and then they were gone.

IKE. Kate, I looked at the flamingos.

KATE. I don't remember.

IKE. I remember I looked because I remember explaining to you that they were pink because of all the crustaceans that they eat.

KATE. I don't remember.

IKE. Do you know that – do you know why flamingos are pink?

ALBIN. I'm not sure that that is actually scientifically the /

KATE. / Yes – but I could have learnt that anywhere.

IKE. Not from him, apparently! (*At* ALBIN.) It is true – bloody look it up!

KATE. Dad?

NESSA. That must have been what you wrote down; your fun fact!

IKE. I looked at the fucking flamingos! I remember it – I can see flamingos in my head – I can see the blue sky and the pink feathers and I can hear the noise of their wings flapping – I can fucking see it, Nessa, so do not tell me I was scribbling.

NESSA. Could he have invented that, Albin – scientifically? Could he have been scribbling and in fact overwritten that scribbling memory with a memory of the sky?

ALBIN. It's possible but /

NESSA. / There we go.

IKE. But what?

ALBIN. There's no way of knowing…

IKE. See.

ALBIN. Either way – not unless someone saw you looking, I mean – there's no way of proving either – unless there's a witness to /

IKE. / Kate?

KATE. I don't remember. Okay?

IKE. Determined to make me out to be an idiot.

KATE. No – I don't remember.

NESSA. She's being generous, Ikey – she's trying to protect you, give her some credit.

KATE. I don't remember.

IKE. Stop calling me Ikey!

KATE. Who cares, it was just a flock –

NESSA. A stand.

KATE. A stand of fucking flamingos.

IKE. Language.

KATE. It was a nice thing to look at – that's all. Now it's not a nice thing. Okay – happy?

IKE. Flamenco.

KATE. What?

IKE. The fact I told you was that the word 'flamingo' comes from the Spanish 'flamenco', meaning fire rather than the fact about the crustaceans –

NESSA. Double bluff, very clever.

KATE. We've killed the fucking flamingos, okay – the flamingos are all dead! Okay?

IKE. Language.

Long pause.

ALBIN. It could feasibly be a case of emotional filtering /

KATE. / Al?

ALBIN. Just quickly – it might be the Adam and Eve syndrome – what fruit was in the Garden of Eden?

NESSA. Apple.

ALBIN. Only became important on the last day – the day they bit it – before that it was just as forgettable as all the other fruits. The notepad, present or not present, may have retrospectively taken on greater significance because it subsequently became important. For example, the first day I met Kate, it wasn't significant at the time, I just met a girl – she could have become any other girl I wasn't going to get to know, I could have walked away and if I had – I wouldn't remember her, the engram wouldn't have lodged. But because subsequently I fell in love with her – that first day got replayed and replayed and is now significant, and thus remembered. You retrospectively add importance – to create a narrative – but at the time it wasn't important at all.

NESSA. I think he's suggesting that we've fallen from grace, Ike, and the whole thing was the fault of your little notebook.

ALBIN. No, what I mean is – you might both be wrong – right – wrong – either; equally. The notebook might not even have – or might as well – not have been there; neither of you cared if it was there at the time.

Beat.

IKE. It wasn't an apple.

ALBIN. What?

IKE. It wasn't an apple in the Garden of Eden.

KATE. Adam and Eve bit the apple.

IKE. The Bible only ever says 'forbidden fruit' – it never says apple, actually – Albin.

NESSA. So it could have been a banana?

ALBIN. Exactly – the apple wasn't even there, it was a metaphor for –

NESSA. Sex gone wrong.

ALBIN. The memory has been rewritten with years and years of misinterpretation.

NESSA. Much like your notebook, Ike.

IKE. And God told them about it right from the get-go – warned them, so it was always significant.

Beat.

KATE. Okay – why don't we play Pictionary?

NESSA. Hey, Al, pink bird, one leg? The beast with two backs?

IKE. Stop calling him Al – it's excruciating.

ALBIN. I don't mind it, it's friendly.

IKE. Careful what you wish for.

KATE. Stop it! Both of you.

NESSA. It's okay, Kate, we're just stretching our legs.

KATE (*stern*). Not in front of my boyfriend you're not, if you
    don't mind.

ALBIN. It's fine.

KATE. It's rude and… unnecessary.

    Beat.

IKE. Chocolate-covered ginger, anyone?

NESSA. Do you remember that bloody Japanese woman that
    wore that face mask? My God, it made me angry – you're in
    the sodding Maasai Mara, the air is practically Brita water-
    filtered – you berk – you do not need a face mask. It was the
    same with eating – at dinner she used to pick over her food
    like a stick insect, just fucking pick it up! Put it in your
    bloody mouth. Take off that bloody face mask – pick up the
    bloody sandwich and stuff the whole thing in your mouth,
    you idiotic tiny woman.

    Pause.

KATE. I'm going to go and have a shower.

NESSA. I was changing the subject.

IKE. To racism?

NESSA. To social observation.

KATE. Al – do you want to go and get the bag from the car?
    And then we'll go to bed.

ALBIN. It's okay, Kate – I don't mind, really.

IKE. You don't like the way the Japanese eat either?

ALBIN. No – I /

KATE. / Shall we go up?

IKE. I've made up your old room – or you can…

KATE. We're fine in my room, thank you.

IKE. Y-yes – I thought so; I just thought, it being adjacent to mine, in case of noise –

NESSA. Noise?

IKE. It's further away from my – privacy – I –

KATE. Okay. Okay – Dad.

IKE. Not – just – you know, you two talking late into the night, nothing – I didn't mean anything else.

ALBIN. I've had a really lovely evening – it's been lovely to meet you both and thank you for dinner, dinner was – delicious. I'm going to go and get the things from the car, are the keys in your bag, Kate – yes – great – I'll go and – do that.

ALBIN *leaves.*

KATE, IKE *and* NESSA *watch him go.*

Beat.

NESSA *collects some cups and glasses.*

NESSA. I'll – make a start on the washing-up.

IKE. I'll turn the hot water on; there are some towels on your bed.

KATE. Thank you.

KATE *exits.*

IKE *and* NESSA *are left alone.*

Silence.

LONDON

KATE *watches* IKE *and* NESSA – *they cannot speak to each other.*

KATE *encourages her mother towards her father.*

KATE (*directly to* IKE). You'd better be getting back –

KELSO

IKE. You'd better be getting back to town – the snow is falling pretty heavily, you'll be hard pushed to get a taxi to come out here as it is.

LONDON

KATE *nudges her mother forward.*

KATE. I'll need to –

KELSO

NESSA (*with real honesty this time, not performative at all, vulnerable almost*). I'll need to stay.

IKE. There's no space.

Beat.

NESSA. It's late and I want to spend some time with Kate, it's been ages since we've all spent time together. I want to get to know Albin, properly.

IKE. Ages? I can tell you how many years – months – days, probably, if you'd like?

NESSA. No – that's okay.

IKE. You can't just… I think it would be better if you stayed in town.

NESSA. Restraint doesn't suit you, Ike. I remember you writing that diary, every night – all those little letters – all those cool,

calm square little letters like tiny little cages, to lock all your
rage into –

NESSA *looks at* IKE *but in doing so looks straight at* KATE,
who still sits outside of the scene as 'writer'.

– to tie up your love. If only you can get it down, get it to sit
down and behave on the page, then it can't hurt you any
more – can it? What do you write in that diary these days?
What's still pulling at the reins, eh, Ike?

IKE. Look – you haven't been here in a long time, why don't
you come back tomorrow – for lunch – because this evening
my daughter and her boyfriend are –

LONDON

KATE. She's ours, ours – straight down the middle.

KELSO

NESSA. She's ours, ours – straight down the middle.

IKE. I didn't leave.

NESSA. When will you stop trying to write bad guys? It's your
weakest suit. They are so two-dimensional – every time.

LONDON

KATE *hands the picture of* NESSA *from* IKE's *desk to* NESSA
– it is as if NESSA *has just found it.*

KELSO

NESSA. Oh. Hello.

NESSA *looks at* IKE. IKE *doesn't say anything.*

I'm young.

IKE. No you're not.

NESSA. In the picture. I'm smiling. This is our honeymoon. I'm smiling.

Pause. It's hugely tender somehow.

IKE. And slim.

NESSA. We stole two bottles of wine from the hotel bar and drank them through straws in the bath.

IKE. Yes.

NESSA. And you gave your penis a beard of bubbles.

IKE. Yes.

NESSA. And I laughed so hard I – farted.

IKE. Yes.

Pause – NESSA puts the photo back down rather respectfully.

NESSA. You should know better, you teach this stuff – the best bad guys are always the ones that still have a little of their humanity left.

ALBIN enters.

IKE. Well, seeing as you are a soulless bitch then you must be a good guy after all – and I'll tell you what my diary doesn't contain, it doesn't contain a comprehensive catalogue of Azerbaijani cock.

NESSA. Hello, Albin.

IKE. Hello.

ALBIN. Hi, guys.

NESSA. Is it awful?

ALBIN. Sorry?

NESSA. The snow.

ALBIN. Still pretty heavy.

IKE. Oh dear.

NESSA. Thank God we're all tucked up inside.

ALBIN. Thank God.

IKE. Can I get you anything?

ALBIN. No – no – I'm fine, thanks.

IKE. Kate's in the shower, she said to say.

ALBIN. When did she go?

IKE. To the shower?

NESSA. Do you want to follow?

ALBIN. I wanted to ask you both something. Whilst I have the chance, with you both –

NESSA. Yes?

ALBIN. Here. I – as Kate's in the shower.

IKE. Right?

LONDON

KATE *stands and watches – she removes her pyjamas and puts her 'Kelso' clothes back on.*

KELSO

KATE *appears in the doorway – she goes to speak but notices the tension and steps back so she can't be seen.*

ALBIN. Um – I – I wondered if, I'm sorry – I – I wondered if you might, mind – (*Breathes deeply.*) agree to – my, me – asking Kate to marry me?

Long pause.

ALBIN *looks at* IKE – *who has seen* KATE.

Kate?

IKE. Kate?

KATE. You didn't turn the hot water on.

IKE. God no, I forgot – one second I'll go and /

ALBIN. / Did you just…

KATE. What?

NESSA. Hear?

KATE. No – what? What were you saying? Mum – did you tell an embarrassing story?

NESSA. No.

KATE. What? Why are you all looking so –

Pause – everyone is aware for the tiniest of moments.

Come on, Al, let's go to bed, we're all tired.

ALBIN. Goodnight. It's been – I've had a nice time.

IKE. It's lovely to meet you, Albin.

NESSA. Yes.

Beat.

IKE. Goodnight, Katy.

KATE. Night, Dad.

IKE. We'll have a lovely breakfast tomorrow, I'll do eggs and croissants and you two just wake up when you're ready –

KATE. We'll leave early.

ALBIN. Sounds – brill, Ike.

KATE and ALBIN exit.

IKE and NESSA left alone. Beat.

NESSA. I'm sorry, I get a bit gobby when I'm nervous.

IKE. Nervous?

NESSA. Yes – very. (*Pause.*) I'm sorry.

IKE. It's just tomorrow. We should make an effort for the sake of –

NESSA. Do you ever feel so proud that we made her? So proud that it makes you –

NESSA *touches her chest lightly with her palm but she can't find the words.*

NESSA *goes to touch* IKE – *not romantically, just a hand on the arm.*

IKE *steps away.*

No response.

Pause.

She's going to marry a lovely man.

IKE. Yes. (*Beat.*) I'll bring you down a duvet.

IKE *exits.*

NESSA *is left looking at the photo of her on the desk.*

NESSA *has lost something.*

Three

LONDON

KATE *sits.*

ALBIN *enters.*

ALBIN. I thought you were coming down.

KATE *turns, almost shocked to see him, and looks up at his face – earnestly.*

You said you were coming down – hours ago.

KATE. I'm sorry.

ALBIN. I'm going to go to bed.

KATE. Right.

Pause.

I need to finish this.

ALBIN. Who is it for?

KATE. Just um – the TV people /

ALBIN. / You've got a show on; they can't expect you to work on press night.

KATE. I'd just rather get it done.

ALBIN. Why did you leave?

Beat.

KATE. I didn't want to watch it. (*Beat.*) It wasn't what I –

Beat.

ALBIN. Are you okay?

KATE. I just need to finish this.

ALBIN. Why?

KATE *doesn't respond.*

What is it?

Beat.

KATE. I just need to…

ALBIN. Your parents are coming tomorrow, we haven't shopped, we haven't done the bedding or – I mean, where are we going to put them?

KATE. I'll sort it.

Beat.

ALBIN. I'm going to bed, Kate.

KATE. Right.

ALBIN. Are you coming?

KATE. I –

ALBIN. Fine.

ALBIN *exits.*

KATE *sits.*

KELSO

ALBIN *enters*.

ALBIN. Weird to think you grew up in here. Little teenage you, all flat-bodied with your hand in your knickers.

KATE (*laughing*). My hand in my what?

ALBIN. You're always going on about what a furious little fiddler you were.

KATE. You're sitting on /

ALBIN. / What?

KATE. You're sitting on Bernard's face.

 ALBIN *gets up and removes a teddy bear from beneath him*.

ALBIN. Bernard?

KATE. Yes – Bernard. Have a little respect; he's been a man in my life for much longer than you have. He's got a bigger bell as well.

ALBIN. What?

KATE. Shake him.

 The teddy makes a jingling sound.

ALBIN. How do you know I don't have a bell – you've never shaken me?

 KATE, *a little downbeat, smiles but doesn't respond*. ALBIN *picks up the bear and puts its face over* KATE's *shoulder – he puts on a sleazy-thigh-rubbing-old-man voice.*

 'Oh, hello, Katy – it's been so long – my, my – haven't you grown into a lovely young lady – I always knew you would – '

 KATE *grabs the bear and pulls it into her lap.*

KATE. Bernard is not a paedophile.

ALBIN. How do you know?

KATE. Because I know bears better than you do.

ALBIN. Your dad said it was a bear then there was a loud noise and the door burst open. I'm a city boy – this is the Borders – how was I meant to know it wasn't a bear?

KATE. Because bears can't open front doors with their paws.

ALBIN. Screw you. Can I – screw you, please?

KATE *smiles.*

Yeah?

KATE. Come on then – 'bear' all.

ALBIN *laughs, starts taking his shirt off, pretending to be a bear.*

ALBIN *crawls towards* KATE, *she laughs and scampers off.*

ALBIN *catches her.*

KATE *goes a little limp – she's stopped playing, she's pensive.*

ALBIN (*stopping*). What?

KATE. Nothing – just – thinking. This room – I – I can't remember anything from before Mum left. I've been trying and there's almost nothing, the odd snapshot, but I think half of them are photos.

ALBIN. You were only ten.

KATE. They must have had sex.

ALBIN. Okay – shirt back on.

KATE. It's just weird – thinking, they must have been in love, once – right? But I can't remember anything from when they were… it's weird. (*Beat.*) I remember this one time, Dad kissing Mum by the fireplace, but it seems really – foreign; like it's someone else, different faces – not my parents. The idea of them holding hands is… I can't remember them ever touching.

ALBIN. Yeah – they don't seem that close.

KATE. You and your powers of perception.

ALBIN *picks up the bear and throws it at* KATE.

Your grandma is so easy and good to be around.

ALBIN. Everyone's family is different.

KATE. I'm sorry they're so –

ALBIN. What?

KATE. Dad – when we arrived, pretending to be on the phone – pretending he was talking to someone.

ALBIN. He was talking to someone.

KATE. No – he does that, he pretends to be on the phone – it's weird, it's –

ALBIN. I think he was on the phone.

KATE. I promise he was /

ALBIN. / I could hear someone on the other /

KATE. / And Mum is so aggressive and insensitive and /

ALBIN. / Stop apologising for them.

KATE. Don't say it like that.

ALBIN. They're your parents.

KATE. Okay.

Beat.

ALBIN. I wasn't telling you off, I just –

KATE. Don't judge me.

ALBIN. I wasn't.

KATE. You don't get it.

ALBIN (*slightly hurt*). No, I guess I don't.

Pause.

KATE. I'm sorry – I'm a dick, I didn't mean that like that.

ALBIN. Being ashamed of your family is kind of – ugly.

KATE. I know.

ALBIN. Well then, don't be.

KATE. It feels like… when I'm here… it all feels really tight
and I feel like I can't swallow. And I want to be light and
laughing and brushing things off but I can't be that – for
some reason. And I just get tighter and tighter – being afraid,
being so horrified by the idea of –

ALBIN. Of what?

KATE. Of getting stuck here.

ALBIN. Stuck?

KATE. The more time I spend here, the more I become a person
that doesn't get on with their parents, and those kinds of
people rarely turn out happy. They aren't good people –
they're messy and… they've failed somehow.

ALBIN. Kate?

KATE. It's ugly.

ALBIN. They love you – you love them, it's not as bad as you
think it is.

KATE. I can't stand it – I can't stand being here, it – it's panic,
it's dread or – the feeling is so big in me, so much bigger
than it should be.

ALBIN. But we had a nice evening, a lovely dinner and they're,
you know – a bit bonkers but /

KATE. / Essentially good people – I know – and I can hardly
breathe. It's wrong – in me, there's something wrong.

ALBIN. Oh.

KATE. I can't stand it when Dad hugs me – he's been a great
dad and he's loved me so much and he's never done anything
– you know – weird – and yet I get really tense every time he
tries to cuddle me… I can't stand it. (*Pause.*) And it's really
– sad.

Pause.

KATE *slumps down on the floor against the bed.* ALBIN
looks down at her.

ALBIN. I don't know what to, um…

KATE. I don't know when it became so difficult. When I was little I used to be so excited about coming back at the end of the school day, we'd put the fire on and have dinner and snuggle on the sofa and in holidays we'd spend days and days in our pyjamas – just me and Dad, just reading or watching films or eating crumpets and it was cosy and – great – and – home. And then – then – something happens and suddenly one time you come back and it looks different, really different, because you – you changed and suddenly you find yourself… judging. It's like you put on these glasses and suddenly a snack isn't a snack because you're hungry, it's a ridiculous fucking parmesan puff that Dad buys to look smart. And you realise that your family – the people you come from, are actually the 'kind of people' that eat parmesan puffs – but you've become the kind of person that thinks the kind of people that eat parmesan puffs are pretentious – but they're still Mum and Dad, right? But you have to laugh at the parmesan-puff people – because if you don't – it's like you don't realise that the parmesan puff actually means wealth and snobbery and social exclusion and weird aspiration – and if you don't *see* that then you're condoning it, you're accepting all that – and I do see – and so I should laugh. But it's still Dad – and – it's what I grew up with so you're actually laughing at your – self – but worse, your own home – you're laughing at your dad – and that's awful and heartbreaking and /

ALBIN. / Or it's just a snack.

Beat.

You grew up, you changed, that's normal /

KATE. / I'm at home and I feel homesick.

ALBIN. Tell them you've changed, explain – they'll understand.

KATE. I don't want to hurt them.

ALBIN. What's the alternative? You keep pretending, you sit here and smile and nod and feel as – much – weird stuff and you're feeling /

KATE. / Weird?

ALBIN. Well, it sounds pretty – intense, Kate. Just tell them…
what's the worst could happen? Eh?

Pause.

KATE*'s face crumples.* ALBIN *stares at her for a moment –
he loves her and he understands. He sits behind her and puts
his arms round her like a little boat, they rock a bit.*

KATE. I love you – so much. You're fucking brilliant.

ALBIN. You're not a monster.

KATE. Thank you.

They nod sincerely.

Beat.

ALBIN (*using Bernard the bear's voice*). 'In fact, Katy, it's been
so long since we hugged, I'd quite like it if you shook my bell.'

KATE. Fuck off, Bernard.

ALBIN. 'Oh, but, Katy – I'm so under-hugged, my stuffing's
gone hard.'

KATE (*laughing*). This is very wrong.

ALBIN. 'Can I give you some stuffing to loosen me up? Will
you shake my bell?'

KATE (*now also using Bernard's voice*). 'I can "bear"-ly
restrain myself.'

ALBIN. 'My Bernard is better than your Bernard.'

KATE. 'Oh, Bernard, you're so meta.'

ALBIN. 'Let me get my paws on you.'

KATE *laughs –* ALBIN *starts kissing her and she rolls back
on her back. They are kissing and laughing – the Bernard
impressions continue. Bernard, on the floor and looking on,
is turned over by one of them so that he can't see
proceedings.* ALBIN *keeps laughing and is making quite a
lot of noise.*

KATE (*sniggering*). Shh –

ALBIN. 'Hear my bear roar!'

KATE (*insistent*). Shh, shh –

ALBIN. 'Look into my beady eyes!'

KATE (*getting tense*). Be quiet!

ALBIN (*unbuttoning her trousers*). 'I'm going to stuff you!'

ALBIN *laughs – it's particularly loud.*

KATE *suddenly stops laughing and moves herself out from under him. The fun is over.*

What?

KATE (*hushes*). I said – be quiet.

ALBIN. What? Why?

KATE. I'm sorry, I – I don't want them to /

ALBIN. / Calm down.

KATE. I'm fine. I don't want them to hear.

ALBIN. We were just laughing – they do know we have sex.

KATE. I know but –

ALBIN. But what?

KATE. It's disrespectful.

ALBIN. Disrespectful?

KATE. Yes.

ALBIN. Come on, you don't really think that? /

KATE. / I'm their little girl.

Pause.

ALBIN *looks at* KATE, *slightly staggered.*

I didn't mean that.

ALBIN. Right.

KATE. I didn't mean that.

ALBIN. I'm going to sleep.

KATE. Al?

ALBIN. I'll keep to my side – I won't touch you, I promise.

> ALBIN *gets in to bed.* KATE *sits at the foot of the bed – pulls her shirt down, rubs her face.*

> KATE *catches sight of Bernard and instinctively pulls him towards herself.*

> KATE *quickly holds him at a distance and looks at him.*

> KATE *pushes Bernard's face hard into the floor.*

> KATE *lifts him up – apologetically, kisses him.* KATE *throws Bernard away.*

LONDON

KATE *sleeps.*

It's the middle of the night.

ALBIN *enters in his boxer shorts and sees* KATE *sleeping.*

ALBIN *puts a blanket over her and exits.*

The sound of ALBIN *exiting rouses* KATE.

KATE *sits and looks at the doorway that* ALBIN *left through.*

KATE *writes.*

Four

KELSO

It's the middle of the night.

ALBIN, *in his boxer shorts, is headed to the toilet – creeping along the landing.*

The landing is pitch black.

ALBIN *suddenly stops – he can hear breathing.*

ALBIN. Hello?

A lighter is lit – and then a cigar.

NESSA. Hello, Albin; doing the midnight creep, are we?

ALBIN. I'm going to the toilet.

NESSA *turns a landing light on – dimly – they can hardly see one another.*

NESSA *is in suspenders and a negligee and smoking a cigar.*

LONDON

KATE *sits dimly in the distance overseeing the scene, cautious of her own imagination – but strangely compelled to keep writing.*

KELSO

NESSA. I realised we didn't give you an answer to your question, earlier.

ALBIN. It's three in the morning /

NESSA. / My answer is no.

ALBIN. Oh.

NESSA. I don't believe in marriage, I wouldn't want my daughter to suffer it.

ALBIN. Right.

NESSA. Romance, yes – lovers – fine – but marriage – no.

ALBIN. Okay. Well – good to know, thank you. I'm going to go to the /

NESSA *steps in* ALBIN*'s path, blowing a little cigar smoke in his way.*

NESSA. / Life is about experience.

ALBIN. Yes.

NESSA. You can only get so much experience from one
person.

LONDON

KATE *stands as if interested to see what* ALBIN *will say next.*

KELSO

ALBIN. I suppose if I were forced to talk this through at three
in the morning – I'd say –

LONDON

KATE. I'd say –

KATE *looks at* ALBIN.

EDIT

ALBIN. I'd say I agree. Look, Nessa – I'm no idealist –
marriage lasts as long as you're happy and then –

ALBIN. I'd say you're probably right.

ALBIN. I'd say I'm not willing to have this conversation with
my mother-in-law.

ALBIN. I'd say nothing is perfect.

ALBIN. I'd say that's the price you pay for not being alone.

ALBIN. I'd say could we talk about this later because I really
do need the toilet.

ALBIN. I'd say – is that an offer?

ALBIN. I'd say – you're right, I've realised Kate is essentially
limiting my freedom and I'm going to move on to green
pastures / pastures new / new ventures / brighter futures –

ALBIN. I'd say – okay –

ALBIN. I'd say –

LONDON

KATE *looks back at the door that* ALBIN *left through – at the blanket he put over her. She's quiet for a moment.*

KATE *looks back to* ALBIN.

KELSO

ALBIN. I'd say that depends on whether you see experience as /

NESSA. / Range? /

ALBIN. / Or depth. I think I see it as depth.

NESSA. Depth, really?

   NESSA *takes a step towards* ALBIN.

ALBIN. You only get to spend fifty years with someone once. Year fifty – knowing what that's like, you only get to do that once. That's a unique experience.

NESSA. Unique enough that you're willing to sacrifice all your independence for it? It's boredom like you can't imagine, resentment that builds, claustrophobia.

   NESSA *takes another step towards* ALBIN – *she places her hand on his chest.*

   ALBIN *doesn't speak – doesn't move.*

   You'll learn.

LONDON

ALBIN *looks at* KATE *a moment, interested as to where she is going to send him next.*

KATE *smiles at* ALBIN.

KELSO

ALBIN *takes her hand off his chest.*

ALBIN. I hope not.

ALBIN *steps past* NESSA.

Goodnight.

NESSA *watches* ALBIN *leave in the twilight.*

LONDON

KATE *sleeps – finally – it's night in the London flat, she's exhausted.*

The night passes and morning comes – the light of dawn fills the office.

KATE *wakes with a start.*

KATE *picks up her phone to check the time.*

KATE *listens to a voicemail.*

ALBIN (*on the voicemail*). Hi – it's me, largely just checking you're alive… I made you some breakfast – and left it –

KATE *lifts up a newspaper and beneath it a cereal bowl – now stodgy – and cup of coffee.*

The review is in, it's there if you want to read it. I've gone to work. (*Beat.*) I don't really understand what's going on… or why you're… (*Beat.*) Anyway – if you're going to keep being Gollum you should probably cancel your parents. I don't want to field it on my own. (*Pause.*) I hope you're okay. Bye. Oh… I love you.

KATE *turns the phone off.*

KATE *picks up the paper to read it.*

KATE *turns to the reviews page.*

KATE *reads a moment…*

KELSO

IKE – *covered top to toe in snow and wearing a large snowsuit – grabs the paper out of* KATE*'s hands and walks across the snow towards the house.*

Five

KELSO

The sitting room.

It is morning – the smell of fresh coffee is coming through from the kitchen.

Everything has been tidied – it is looking lovely again.

The sitting room is silent.

KATE *and* ALBIN *enter with their bags, ready to go.*

They listen. Beat. They can't hear anything.

ALBIN. Got everything?

KATE. Just need to grab my iPhone charger from the kitchen –

ALBIN. I got it last night.

KATE. We should say goodbye.

ALBIN. Course.

> *The front door opens and in walks* IKE, *in his ski-gear, with a serious pair of snow shoes on; he's covered in the stuff, he's carrying the paper.*

KATE. Dad?

IKE (*brushing off*). Morning, all – how are we?

ALBIN. Good thanks. Been out, have you?

IKE. Funny.

KATE. What are you doing?

IKE. Car wouldn't start, wanted the paper.

KATE. What?

IKE. What are the bags for, you can't be leaving already?

KATE. We need to be back to Edinburgh by /

IKE. / But you've barely arrived.

ALBIN. I'm sorry we –

IKE. I haven't seen you in months.

KATE. I'm sorry – we'll – we'll have a cup of tea.

IKE. I'll put some breakfast on.

KATE. I think Mum is /

IKE. / She better not be in my bloody kitchen.

> NESSA *blustering in from the kitchen – she is a picture of domestic bliss, pinny, flour on her face, maybe even singing a tune.*

NESSA. Morning, darling – s – how are you? Did you sleep alright? I've made some fresh croissants – quite a success – I tell you, thought I'd forgotten.

IKE. Bloody hell.

NESSA. Language, dear.

IKE. It's the hospitable undead.

NESSA. Sit yourself down and get comfortable – the coffee is just brewing, I'll bring it through.

KATE. Just a quick one before we shoot.

NESSA. Albin?

ALBIN. Yes.

NESSA. Coffee?

ALBIN. Thanks.

> NESSA *raises her eyes at him.*
>
> ALBIN *smiles tightly.*

NESSA *exits back through to the kitchen.*

IKE *dusts himself down and sits with the paper.*

We might as well – sit?

KATE *reluctantly puts down the bags and settles in – a little awkwardly.*

How the Rangers doing in the third division?

IKE. The Rangers? Of where?

ALBIN. Not to worry.

KATE. Football, Dad.

IKE. Oh, right – yes – Queen's Park Rangers.

ALBIN. Glasgow.

IKE. They played there? This week?

ALBIN. Um –

NESSA *blusters back in with coffee and croissants.*

NESSA. Here we go. Milk?

IKE. Yes, please.

NESSA. Albin – a croissant?

ALBIN. Thanks.

NESSA. No chance we could turn the radio down just a smidgen? Seem to have a bit of a headache.

IKE. Must be the snow, dear.

NESSA. Must be the snow.

Radio 4 plays – the snow falls, IKE *reads the paper,* NESSA *hands out refreshments. For a few moments, it looks a lot like a homely country idyll.* ALBIN *quickly acclimatises, although slightly wary of* NESSA, *he sits with croissant, coffee, section of the paper.*

IKE. It's in here.

KATE. Yes.

IKE. Bloody hell – look at that, it's in here. Oh – oh! Look – oh! There's a little side bar with a bit about Kate.

KATE *sits very still trying not to be tense.*

NESSA. Oh, let me look – oh, oh – let me look. Oh, look, there's a picture!

ALBIN. There's a picture?

ALBIN *goes to stand to try and look at the paper.*

KATE *catches him and pulls him back down into the chair.*

NESSA. Oh, darling – haven't they made you look clever?

IKE. Shush – I'm reading.

NESSA. Very bookish. Was that shirt their idea or yours? It's very bookish. (*Looks up from the paper at* KATE.) Oh, look – you're wearing it now, how funny. Look – flatten your hair and look a bit grumpy – it looks just like you!

KATE. It is me.

IKE. Stop mauling it – I'm trying to read it.

NESSA. Read it out.

KATE. No – really, I've read it.

NESSA. Go on – read it out, I want to hear it read.

KATE. Honestly – Dad – please don't. It doesn't matter.

ALBIN *reaches to get another croissant and by mistake brushes* NESSA.

NESSA *turns to look at him –* ALBIN *immediately sits back in his chair, nervous.*

NESSA. Al, you want to hear it, don't you?

KATE. I've read it – why don't you two read it between you.

IKE. This is brilliant – Kate, this is so brilliant.

NESSA. Read it, Ike! Read it! Al – you want to hear it, don't you?

ALBIN. Um – I'm not really /

KATE. / No. He doesn't.

NESSA. Don't be shy.

KATE. I'm not being shy. I'm asking you to please not –

NESSA. Don't be precious.

KATE. I'm not being precious.

IKE *stands up, proud as punch, and rests his glasses on the end of his nose. He holds the paper high up in front of him and clears his throat, it's quite the performance.*

IKE. Okay – '*Tramlines* – Bane's charming satire of a West London Tennis Club – is as quaint as it is quirky, serving up laughter and tears in equal bouts. Whilst a little tame in parts and occasionally hackneyed in its attempts at class satire, Bane's razor-sharp wit – delivered by Bainbridge and McCartney's captivatingly comic performances – is coupled with an impressively academic understanding of tennis to make for an entertaining evening.'

KATE *stands and rips the paper from* IKE*'s hands.*

Beat.

I was just /

KATE. / I'm sorry – I'm very sorry, I don't want to read it.

IKE. It's three stars.

KATE. I know what it says.

NESSA. Don't be so ungrateful.

IKE. Three stars is good.

KATE. I'm pleased, I'm pleased for the review, I'm pleased for the success – I'm grateful and I'm pleased.

IKE. Then what's the problem with reading it out?

KATE *looks back at* ALBIN.

Beat.

KATE *doesn't speak.*

NESSA. Don't sulk.

KATE. I'm not sulking.

IKE. What's wrong with it?

KATE. Please.

IKE. Come on – spit it out.

KATE. Please. Don't.

Beat.

IKE. I'd like to know why our being proud of you is so unbearable?

Beat.

KATE. I'm glad you're proud, I just – don't want to –

IKE. What's wrong with the play?

KATE. It doesn't *do* anything.

IKE. Do?

KATE. I find it difficult – this… difficult.

Pause.

IKE. Difficult? It's a good review.

KATE. Thank you.

IKE. I know people that would give their eye teeth to get a review like that.

Pause.

KATE *looks at* IKE.

ALBIN. Perhaps we should listen to the radio?

NESSA. No – no, Albin, they're trying to have a fight.

KATE. No we're not.

Pause – KATE and IKE back down, and carry on with breakfast in silence.

IKE. I've read it, I loved it – I think it's brilliant. I told my students to read it.

KATE. Thank you.

IKE. But you don't think it's good?

Pause – KATE *doesn't respond.*

So you know better?

KATE. No.

NESSA. Ike?

IKE. No, I'm interested, creatively – in this – I think it's great and you think it doesn't *do* anything?

KATE. It's not very honest. (*Beat.*) I feel – I feel it isn't very honest.

Pause.

ALBIN *gives* KATE *the coffee.*

Thank you.

IKE. Can you use a coaster, please?

KATE *takes a coaster and puts it underneath her cup.*

NESSA. I can make more croissants – dig in.

IKE. Do you think that *I'm* not very honest?

Pause – KATE *looks at her father.*

KATE. Your name is Iain.

IKE. What?

KATE. Your name isn't Ike, it is Iain.

IKE. What's that got to do with anything?

KATE. I don't know why you changed your name.

NESSA. It's started snowing again.

IKE. I preferred Ike.

NESSA. It's really coming down.

ALBIN. I like Ike.

KATE. You said this was a good idea, you said if I explained they would understand – you said don't underestimate them.

ALBIN. Did I?

KATE. Yes.

NESSA. Albin has the real measure of us, knows we're made of tougher stuff – don't you – Al?

Beat.

ALBIN. I – I just think generally if everyone is completely honest then nothing can ever be that bad; for what it's worth.

NESSA. Oh, what a good family policy, let's play.

ALBIN. It's not a game.

NESSA. Sorry – my mistake. I'll start: Albin invited me.

KATE. What?

ALBIN. Oh, wow.

IKE. You invited Nessa here?

ALBIN. We were meant to meet in Edinburgh – tomorrow, but she – you just –

NESSA. Arrived.

IKE. Of course you did.

KATE. Meet?

ALBIN. All three of us.

KATE. How?

ALBIN. I emailed her.

KATE. What? How did you get her email address?

ALBIN. I – stole it from your computer. I wanted it to be a surprise.

KATE. 'Surprise: I breached your trust.'

ALBIN. I'm sorry – I –

NESSA. Oh, calm down, I think it's rather endearing, romantic.

IKE. You would.

NESSA. Albin was being responsible, proactive, because he wanted to talk to us about something.

Silence – neither KATE *nor* ALBIN *want to hear what comes next.*

Have we stopped playing?

KATE. It's not a game.

Their silence shuts NESSA *down immediately, she smiles – almost pleased.*

Pause.

IKE *goes to pour himself a cup of coffee. The* Desert Island Discs *music plays in the background.*

IKE (*suddenly exploding*). What the fuck has my changing my name got to do with your bloody play?

KATE *can't speak – she's silent.*

NESSA. I think she's calling you a fraud, Ike – I think she's saying you're bound to like her silly fraudulent play because you are a silly fraud.

ALBIN. That's not honesty – that's antagonism.

NESSA. You are calling him a fraud, aren't you? Honestly – aren't you?

KATE. No – I'm not – I'm trying to explain that /

IKE. / I'm a fraud, Kate?

KATE. No – that's not –

IKE. Am I a fraud for liking your play? Does it take a fraud to enjoy it – is that what you're saying?

KATE. I thought I'd written something in – in opposition, I thought I'd written against the… I thought I'd written something important – but instead the very people I tried to oppose came along and bought their tickets and had a jolly good laugh. They just laughed and laughed. They were entertained.

IKE. People like me? Frauds – like me?

KATE. Dad –

IKE. You sat in that theatre as a child, begged me to take you – you sat there with your mouth open and your eyes glistening – in – wonder.

KATE. I know.

IKE. You thought it was magic.

KATE. I know.

IKE. And now you've, what? Got contempt for it? Risen above it?

KATE. No.

IKE. Am I a fraud for being entertained, Kate?

KATE. I just wish you could see that that isn't the, wasn't the – point.

IKE. I'm the fraud? *I'm* the fraud – when Lady fucking Muck over there is swinging around the southern hemisphere pretending to be Bilbo fucking Baggins, understanding the 'real poor' – whilst her family are paying her fucking rent! I'm the fraud?

ALBIN. Again, that's antagonism rather than – it's best to try and stay calm rather than /

IKE. / I grew up in one of the roughest schemes in Dundee, young lady – I had a youth that you, you wouldn't even begin to cope with /

KATE. / And now you won't shop in Tesco; you won't even go in there because you're afraid of catching poor, of being caught and dragged back down.

IKE. Don't you dare speak to your father like that!

NESSA. Calm down, Ike – the game requires staying calm.

KATE. We're not real people, we're pretending – we're parmesan fucking pretending!

ALBIN. It's not a game.

KATE. If you ever bothered to go and see your mum, and
brought her to see my play, she wouldn't be able to stomach
it – and if you went to get her wearing that fucking cardigan
you'd get five shades of shit kicked out of you before you
even got to your own front door. You'd look like a stranger in
the house you grew up in. So do not be appalled at me for
trying to tell you that I feel different to where I came from. I
am trying not to pretend… because I don't want to be
pretend, because pretend people aren't very easy to love or to
live with. The play is pretend – coasters – (*Picks up the
coaster.*) are fucking pretend.

KATE *tries hard to snap the coaster and it doesn't break.*
KATE *throws down the coaster.*

IKE. You're wrong.

KATE. Am I?

IKE. Granny would laugh. She'd sit and she'd laugh – because
it's entertaining.

Pause.

KATE. Entertaining isn't the point.

IKE. Well then, I guess Granny isn't the point.

NESSA *goes over to the sideboard and gets out the whisky.*

Nessa – it's fucking eleven o'clock in the morning.

NESSA. Keep your eye on your own balls, Ike. Albin?

NESSA *pours herself a whisky.*

ALBIN. Coffee for me – thanks. Kate – why don't we go for a
walk?

IKE. And as for my being a 'fraud', Kate – I'd like to remind
you that the only reason you are able to put together such a
cogent accusation, the only reason you know the fucking
word 'fraud' is because I am not on that scheme, and so you
are not on that scheme. I paid with hard fucking work for
you to have the free time to acquire a thorough
understanding of the concept of 'fraudulence' amongst other
high-minded ideas, Kate. And let me tell you – you sure as

fuck wouldn't be writing plays at all if you were still living
with Granny and the rest of the 'real' people.

KATE. Jayde did.

NESSA. Who the hell is Jade?

KATE. Jayde – with a y –

NESSA. Ugh.

KATE. Has something to say for herself – because nobody owns
her words, do they, Dad? She's still allowed to speak because
no one paid for her ideas. Isn't that right? Pure gold just
sings out the middle of her.

IKE. You want to be worse off?

KATE. No.

IKE. You ungrateful little –

KATE. You can have ideas without having to pay for them.

IKE. Yours just happen to have been bought with my money –
but you could have done it another way?

KATE. You did – you dragged yourself up!

NESSA. He married himself up.

IKE. I worked hard.

NESSA. You fucked hard.

ALBIN. Whoa.

NESSA. Honestly. He did.

ALBIN. Okay.

KATE. How much? How much do I have to pay back before
I'm free to have an opinion? And how do I do that? Tell me,
how much hard labour? How much do I have to pay back
before I can be something other than grateful? Hm? Before
I'm allowed to criticise?

NESSA. I don't think you're having too much trouble as it is,
darling.

IKE. Listen to you! Standing there preaching with some lefty fervour fuelled by good fucking coffee that I bought with my hard work because I know you won't touch the instant stuff. Do you drink instant coffee, Kate?

KATE. I don't drink instant coffee because we never had it.

NESSA. She's not wrong.

KATE. The only time you'd buy it is when we had builders working in the house and even then you'd put it on a separate little tray with the shit cups with the cracks in and tell me not to drink it.

IKE. We never told you to drink the good wine; you cracked on to that all on your own.

KATE. I must have had a taste for it – it was probably in my breast milk.

NESSA. Now – that's unfair.

IKE. That bottle we had last night cost the best part of forty quid and you didn't even flinch. Albin here had the decency to say 'that's a nice bottle' /

ALBIN. / I sort of meant the label. I don't know anything about /

IKE. / But you – you glugged it right on down – a forty-quid bottle of wine that you're so used to drinking that it goes down like fucking Ribena! And gives you a sore enough head to wake up and accuse me of elitism.

KATE *spits the coffee out all over* IKE.

KATE. I don't want it!

ALBIN (*quietly*). Oh, fuck.

IKE. What next? Take all your clothes off? Jacket, boots – I'm pretty sure we paid for the posture as well so we'll have that back – let's have the teeth as well – few thousand went in there and if you still manage to shoot your spoilt little mouth off with no teeth – we'll see how you do minus the tongue – you may think you now *see* the world and *see* me as an idiot but I'd like to remind you – the vocabulary, the articulacy, the accent, the education and even the fucking orthodontistry were all paid for by the empty, meaningless and fraudulent value system that you are so eloquently rejecting, young lady. So please – I beg of you – stop wagging your finger at us with one hand whilst stuffing your face with dauphinois fucking potatoes with the other. Okay?

Beat.

KATE. What eight-year-old turns down extra potatoes if they're yummy? You fed it to me.

IKE. You ate it.

KATE *exits.*

Pause.

ALBIN *is left standing with* IKE *and* NESSA.

IKE *pours himself a glass of whisky and stands with his back to* ALBIN *and* NESSA *whilst he drinks it.*

NESSA. I don't think your game worked very well, Albin.

ALBIN. It's not a game.

NESSA. Apparently not.

ALBIN. She was trying to explain.

NESSA. I suppose you don't have all this?

ALBIN. What?

NESSA. You've suffered – I mean, losing your parents at that age – you really suffered; so you're bound to have something interesting to say. That's a story I'd be convinced by.

ALBIN *stares at her, speechless.*

Maybe Kate should bump us off – or have something ghastly happen to us… I'm going to make some more croissants, do join me if you fancy.

NESSA *smiles at* ALBIN. *It's strangely kind – completely honest – refreshing almost.*

ALBIN *nods a little.*

IKE *pours another whisky and hands it to* ALBIN.

IKE. I'd be delighted, delighted if you joined the family; I didn't get the chance to say – you have my blessing.

ALBIN *takes the whisky.*

ALBIN. Thanks.

IKE. Will be good to have another man about the place; some more skin in the game.

ALBIN *nods at* IKE, *who collapses, exhausted, into an armchair.*

ALBIN *knocks back the whisky – nods.*

You should go and –

ALBIN. Yep, yeah. (*Beat.*) Ike?

IKE. Yes?

ALBIN. Would you like me to call you Iain?

IKE. No.

ALBIN. Right. Okay.

ALBIN *exits.*

Six

KELSO

KATE's *bedroom.*

KATE *sits on the bed.*

ALBIN *enters a little hesitantly.*

ALBIN. Hi.

KATE. Hey.

Beat.

ALBIN. I've started the car; the windscreen is just defrosting then we can /

KATE. / Leave. (*Pause.*) You can come in; you don't have to stand at the door.

ALBIN *stays in the doorway.*

ALBIN. Staying outside your projectile range.

KATE. I just spat at my dad.

ALBIN. Yes – yes you did.

KATE. I just spat at my dad and then stormed off to my bedroom. I'm thirty years old – I was on the brink, in there somewhere I was genuinely on the verge of going – (*Puts her tongue inside her bottom lip and going 'uuuuhhh'.*)

ALBIN. You should have pulled a chinny on him.

KATE. What?

ALBIN. You know, rubbing your chin – the beard thing.

KATE. Oh, yeah. (*Whilst doing the chinny.*) Sure – sure, Al – yeah – sure?

ALBIN. Uf – don't, makes me want to punch you.

They laugh a moment.

Come on, let's go home.

KATE. I can't.

Beat.

ALBIN. What?

KATE. I need to not just – leave. You said to try and make them understand.

ALBIN. Didn't work.

KATE. No.

ALBIN. Let's go. It's started snowing again, if we don't get a move on we'll /

KATE. / Less than twenty-four hours and he's gone from 'let's play happy families' – to 'no thanks, too much bother, let's bail.'

ALBIN. That's not what I said.

KATE. Remind me not to get on sinking ships with you, Al.

ALBIN. Kate – this isn't bailing, this is a sensible attempt at salvage; this is damage limitation.

KATE. It's running away.

ALBIN. I don't want to be part of this!

KATE. You think I do? I feel uncomfortable and threatened and –

ALBIN. Well then let's fucking go!

KATE. It's my family – I need to resolve /

ALBIN. / What? What are you going to resolve? What are you going to find? You think *that* fucking show – was catharsis? You think we're all going to stretch this out and shake hands? Your mum just told me I was lucky that my parents died, that I should write a fucking book about it. You just spat at your dad – I think we should take a breather before we reconvene.

KATE. You're overreacting.

ALBIN. I want to go home!

KATE. Well go then.

Pause – ALBIN *paces the room.*

ALBIN *doesn't leave.*

Leaving – means I'm not alright with where I'm from and – that's just like Dad – that's history repeating and the whole thing happens all over again.

ALBIN. This isn't some mythology – it's not causal – it's not a story – it's three people shouting at each other, Kate.

KATE. No.

ALBIN. It's us, Kate – it's not them – we're a new thing, we're a team – you and me, a little unit, we front it together, we make our own roots.

KATE. Two people aren't enough.

ALBIN. What?

KATE. Families need history, context – it's what makes them strong.

ALBIN (*pointing downstairs*). Hey, kids – let's go and see Granny and Grandpa they can tell us about all the old stories; the one where Granny tells Grandpa that he fucked hard and the one where Mummy spat at Grandpa – and the one where Grandma tried to seduce Daddy in the middle of the night.

KATE. What?

ALBIN. Last night – your mother came on to me. Now – please – can we go home?

Beat.

KATE. She always does that.

ALBIN. What?

KATE. She does that to all my boyfriends.

ALBIN. That's meant to make me feel better?

KATE. It's just a thing she does, she doesn't mean it.

ALBIN. She meant it.

KATE. No she didn't.

ALBIN. Trust me – she meant it.

KATE. You are resistible, you know.

ALBIN. This isn't fucking arrogance; this is horror – I'm fucking scarred.

KATE. You didn't give in, did you?

ALBIN. No! Fuck's sake –

KATE. Well then.

ALBIN. 'Well then'? Says the girl that won't have sex in her parents' house because she's their 'little girl'?

KATE. It just a thing Mum does.

ALBIN. This is fucked up – this family is fucked up!

KATE. They're my family – they're my parents and I love them. You are in their home and you have no right, absolutely no right to judge them. They brought me up well – they made me who I am and if you love me then you should respect them.

ALBIN (*flabbergasted*). The hypocrisy is –

KATE. They are my parents!

ALBIN. I don't want this. I can't handle this /

KATE. / You wanted in when you thought it was easy, invite Mum – have a few parmesan puffs – ask them to be your parents too – eh?

ALBIN. What?

KATE. I heard you talking to them; it's why you got Mum here. You wanted to –

ALBIN. Don't, don't do that – I only get to do that once – do not do that like that. Don't.

Pause.

KATE. I'm sorry.

Pause.

ALBIN *is seething.*

ALBIN. You're using my proposal as fucking leverage and I haven't even made it yet – you stole it, you fucking stole it and made it a weapon – you cow.

KATE. I'm really sorry – that was –

ALBIN. It's the kind of thing your mother would do. Yeah – fucking have that, Goldilocks.

KATE. Al?

ALBIN. I'm angry – I'm really fucking angry you just did that.

KATE. Okay – I know – but talking about it any more is just going to take more chunks out of it so –

KATE *goes to touch* ALBIN.

ALBIN *pulls away.*

ALBIN. Exactly. Let it recover, leave it alone. (*Beat.*) Let's go home.

Pause.

KATE. I need to know what they did wrong.

ALBIN. What difference does it make – to now, to us?

KATE. I need to know which bit to cut out of me so that we can be happy.

ALBIN. You aren't them.

Beat.

KATE. Do you really believe it's possible – for it to last… for ever?

ALBIN. Yes, yes I do.

KATE. I've never seen it work; not aunts or uncles or grandparents, not one set of my friends' parents are still together – you watch fifty people get in a car and the car crashes every time – you don't get in the fucking car. That's not cynicism; it's logic.

ALBIN. Good metaphor.

KATE. I'm sorry – I – I didn't mean /

ALBIN. / It isn't evidence that makes you sure.

Pause – ALBIN *looks at* KATE.

Beat.

ALBIN *exits.*

KATE. Al? (*Beat.*) Al?

KATE *is left alone.*

KATE *stares at the room as if it might produce some sort of answer.*

She suddenly stands and moves a chair to fetch a box down from the top shelf of one of the cupboards.

The box is full of photographs, trinkets, old birthday cards and five or six notebooks, bursting with ticket stubs and the scrawling writing of a teenage girl.

KATE *starts flicking furiously through the diaries in search of some piece of evidence, some sentence that will confirm things for her –* KATE *stops at a page and reads.*

Seven

LONDON

It's late in the evening – KATE *is exhausted – she finishes the scene – she puts the pen down.*

KATE *looks around the office – she is alone.*

ALBIN *has not returned from work.*

KATE *checks her watch.*

KATE (*shouts down the stairs*). Al? Al?

No response.

KATE *turns from the door.*

MEMORY

KATE *is twelve with a suitcase in her hand – she's leaving the house to holiday with* NESSA.

IKE *stands at the door.*

IKE. Are you off, then? Ready to go, eh? Have a good time with your mother. No, no, I'll be fine on my own; don't be silly. Have fun. I love you… very much.

IKE *waves* KATE *off – he smiles – he's pleased.*

MEMORY

KATE *is twelve with a suitcase in her hand – she's leaving the house to holiday with* NESSA.

IKE *stands at the door.*

IKE. Are you off, then? Ready to go, eh? Have a good time with your mother. No, no, I'll be fine on my own; don't be silly. Have fun. I love you… very much.

IKE *waves* KATE *off – he's desperately trying to hold back tears.*

MEMORY

IKE. Have fun. I love you… very much.

IKE *waves* KATE *off – he smiles – he's pleased.*

IKE. Have fun. I love you… very much.

IKE *waves* KATE *off – he's desperately trying to hold back tears.*

IKE. Have fun. I love you… very much.

IKE *waves* KATE *off – he smiles – he's pleased.*

IKE. Have fun. I love you… very much.

IKE *waves* KATE *off – he's desperately trying to hold back tears.*

KELSO

KATE *turns on* IKE.

KATE. Nothing has moved in this room, Dad.

IKE *stops in the doorway.*

Nothing has moved. It's all in exactly the same position, all the photos and these stupid plate things are all in exactly the same place, it's like a museum or a crime scene or a fucking –

KATE *picks up a small glass trinket, contained within it are her milk teeth.*

IKE. Be careful.

KATE. Why are you still here? Why don't you move – go somewhere new and paint the walls white, I'd help you move, we'd help you paint the walls – if you moved.

IKE. Don't break that.

KATE. Mum was fine – Mum survived – unscarred – she's free and happy and she made herself happy. She's seen so much and travelled – she's got a life and – and – she's done things – she got up and – she forgot about it. She fucking survived!

IKE. I said – be careful!

KATE. You could have got up and – and – you could have recovered, you could have made yourself happy.

IKE *steps away – to leave.*

You didn't have to be the victim – it didn't have to destroy you. Dad? Dad?

IKE *doesn't move.*

KATE *throws the small glass jar and it smashes on the ground.*

KATE *looks at the mess on the floor.*

IKE *stays in the doorway – back turned.*

MEMORY

NESSA (*interested in her daughter*). Darling! Darling! Look at you – turn around – look at you. Let me take your bags. How was the flight? Was it long? We are going to have such a

glorious time, just you wait – India is the land of adventure.
We will wear saris and go on trips and eat the most exotic
foods – are you excited? Are you excited? Are you ready? I
have to finish talking to a friend for just two minutes – so
wait here – and then we're off – just two minutes – okay, you
wait here – and then we're off! (*Pause.*) Yes, darling?

MEMORY

NESSA (*distracted*). Are you ready? I have to finish talking to a
friend for just two minutes – so wait here – and then we're
off – just two minutes – okay, you wait here – and then we're
off! Yes, darling?

LONDON

KATE *stands at looks at her mother, replaying the memory –
unsure of the interpretation.*

MEMORY

NESSA (*interested*). Yes, darling?

NESSA (*distracted*). Yes, darling?

NESSA (*interested*). Yes, darling?

NESSA (*distracted*). Yes, darling?

KELSO

NESSA *enters in a kimono – breezy from the bath – rubbing
oils into her hands.*

KATE. When were you happiest?

Pause – NESSA *thinks a moment.*

NESSA. When I was in Nepal, in Kathmandu – there is an
amazing food market called Asan Tole – in the mornings I
would wake up at sunrise, when the city was just coming to
life and the air felt fresh – I'd take my book and walk to this

little café on the corner of the market run by my friend
Sunita. She worked there alone in the mornings – before her
father arrived, lazy sod never turned up before ten – and she
would serve me vegetable-and-potato soup –

KATE. For breakfast?

NESSA. Mm-hm – and the most delicious milk tea you have
ever tasted. And Sunita and I would sit on stools with our
feet up and watch the market unpack – and talk and talk.

KATE. What about?

NESSA. Everything, how we felt, what we thought – nothing
was off-limits. The kind of talking that you do with only very
good girlfriends – the kind that makes you feel… full.

KATE. Yeah.

NESSA. And there was this one little man called Bibek who ran
the stall opposite and he was so in love with Sunita – and
every morning as he unpacked his nuts –

KATE. Blimey.

NESSA *hits* KATE *on the shoulder affectionately.*

NESSA. He was a nut seller. He would stick his bum out and
pull his sleeves up over his biceps and sing these funny songs
about 'the pretty girl in the café' and think we didn't notice.
It used to crack us up… we laughed until we pee'd.

KATE *laughs.*

KATE. Did she ever get together with him?

NESSA. No – she was far too happy to become a wife.

Small beat.

KATE. What does that mean?

NESSA. Nothing – it was a joke /

KATE. / Do you think I should marry Albin?

Beat.

NESSA. I think the fact you have reservations is a good sign.

KATE. Why?

Beat.

NESSA. Because you're smart. Because you've worked hard to work out who you are and what you want and you realise that...

KATE. That what?

Beat.

NESSA. That marriage compromises your – self.

KATE. I don't know if I agree.

NESSA. Really?

NESSA *looks at* KATE, KATE *avoids* NESSA*'s gaze.*

Your ambition blunts a little – your confidence is... eroded.

KATE. I don't want to hear this.

Pause.

NESSA. I remember being your age. Me and my girlfriends as we started creeping towards thirty and, I mean, we were a very independent bunch – we were self-aware – and we were reaching this age where marriage and babies were expected and it /

KATE. / You didn't have to do it.

NESSA. It wasn't the social expectation that was the problem, we wanted it – I wanted it – the house, the kids... it was the first time in my life I wanted something and I wasn't able to get it just by working hard. A whole life of self-development, hard work to earn your choices and then suddenly, overnight, men had become these cardholders that could make or break our lives by breaking up with us at the wrong time because our wombs had a sell-by date. The implicit inequality of that, the shock of that injustice – caused by our own bodies – was... horrifying. (*Pause.*) And I don't know how it happens – but that status imbalance somehow works its way into the foundations of a marriage.

KATE. Your marriage maybe – but not every marriage.

NESSA. I believe that in every marital home the female sense
of self suffers from erosion more than the male.

KATE. What? I should just never get married, then?

NESSA. You can get married; just know that you will disappear
a little; I wasn't willing to accept that.

KATE. This feels horrible.

NESSA. I'm trying to protect you. Give you options.

KATE. The option to be alone?

NESSA. You're never alone, friendship, lovers – enhance you –
make you stronger – marriage is /

KATE. / Al and I – we're friends, we talk – we're not enemies,
it's not a war. We're equal. I know it's going to be hard but /

NESSA. / How hard?

KATE. Hard.

NESSA. Hard enough you might be unhappy?

KATE. Sometimes.

NESSA. For how long?

KATE. As long as it takes.

NESSA. Well, sooner or later that's not hard, that's just unhappy.

Pause.

KATE *looks at her mother in askance – as if she has seen
something new.*

KATE. What was Dad's choice?

Pause – NESSA *looks at her shoes.*

EDIT

KATE. Dad didn't have a choice.

KATE. Dad could have got up and – and – left – he could have
recovered, he could have made himself happy. Could he?

KELSO

KATE. What was Dad's choice? Mum – what was Dad's choice?

KATE *sees the teeth at her feet – scattered on the floor.*

KATE *bends down to pick up the teeth.*

Beat.

What is that?

IKE. They're your teeth.

KATE *picks up one tooth – it's tiny – she holds it in her palm.*

Beat.

Why did you bring Albin here?

KATE. I wanted to show him…

IKE. What?

KATE. Where I grew up.

Beat.

IKE *bends down to start collecting the smashed pieces of the jar.*

Dad, don't – I'll do it –

IKE *waves* KATE *away, it's almost aggressive –* KATE *steps back.*

IKE. The past takes looking after, Kate. You can't just pop by for cosy weekends that feel like home without someone doing the upkeep in-between – history is earned, worked for – kept by people.

KATE. But I don't want you to have to /

IKE. / I want you to feel that you come from somewhere, because when that goes, when you throw that away – you start floating and you never come back down and it… fundamentally undermines you, for ever; and I don't want you to struggle with that.

KATE. But not if it means you're – stuck.

IKE. Even if it means, I'm stuck.

KATE. But I only come home twice a year it's /

IKE. / Well, visit more often.

KATE. I don't want to feel responsible for /

IKE (*belts it*). / Have you got any idea how hard it's been!

KATE *turns away from* IKE.

MEMORY

KATE *is twelve with a suitcase in her hand – she's leaving the house to holiday with* NESSA.

IKE *stands at the door.*

IKE. Are you off, then? Ready to go, eh? Have a good time with your mother. No, no, I'll be fine on my own; don't be silly. Have fun. I love you… very much.

IKE *waves* KATE *off – he's desperately trying to hold back tears.*

KELSO

KATE *turns on* NESSA.

NESSA. These things are complicated, Kate – it's never a case of /

KATE. / You think it's your duty to warn me about disappointment?

NESSA. I'm just telling you what I wish I'd /

KATE. / Do you think a ten-year-old having to deal with a forty-year-old man that is falling apart, crying in the night and barely able to haul himself through the days but sucking it up and doing it anyway – do you think that ten-year-old still needs warning about disappointment?

NESSA *doesn't respond.*

Do you?

NESSA. It's not my fault that the institution is flawed, I know it's upsetting, I know you want to believe, but –

KATE. There are plenty of people who make it work.

NESSA. I'm just trying to tell you what I wish my mother had told me.

KATE. Maybe she kept her mouth shut so you could muster enough courage to give it a shot.

NESSA. I don't want to lie to you.

KATE. Crusts make your hair go curly and if you eat sweets you'll shrink, carrots make you see in the dark, your eyes will go square and your face will stay that way.

NESSA. There are plenty of truths I protect you from, darling, but not this one – this one is too important.

KATE. Protect me? From what – what don't I know? What don't I know?

Beat.

NESSA. Being with someone who can't be comfortable with where they're from – they itch – itch and burn and burn until you've scratched so hard that you go see-through – you scratch a big hole in the middle of you – the kind of hole that no one can ever love you enough to fill – that isn't the kind of mess someone wants to stay married to. Your father and I were never comfortable with where we were from – the fear of becoming our parents – got right into bed between us – and six people is too many people to have in a bed and be comfortable. That's what I owe you – telling you that.

Long pause.

KATE. This is going to hurt.

IKE. Right.

KATE. I know you love me.

IKE. That doesn't hurt.

KATE. I sometimes find it very hard to be around you, very very hard. I don't look forward to it – it feels like a /

IKE. / Okay.

KATE. And I don't think it's your fault, I don't – know – but I know you love me and you've been a brilliant dad so – it can't be your fault.

IKE. Right.

KATE. Which makes it my fault or something in me – something wrong in me and the feeling of not wanting to be here is sometimes such a big feeling that it feels very wrong. And I don't know when it happened or why but I used to love to hug you and now I find it very difficult and I'd like to fix that.

Silence.

IKE *steps forward to hug* KATE.

KATE *steps backwards.*

IKE. Why do you think it might be?

Long pause.

KATE. I'm terrified of becoming you.

Beat.

IKE (*drawing breath – soldiering on*). Why?

KATE. I don't want to be left on my own.

IKE *exits.*

NESSA *exits.*

LONDON

KATE *sits in the office on her own.*

Eight

KELSO

KATE *goes back to the box that she found her diaries in, she rootles around, starts pulling things out – old lipsticks, trinkets, medals.* KATE *looks at the debris. She then, with some fervour, starts pulling more boxes down from shelves – clearing out what is under her bed, pulling it all out and scattering it everywhere. She puts Bernard up high so he can watch things.* KATE *finds a book of old photos – sticks a few of them up on the wall. She finds certificates, birthday cards – a large poster of Leonardo di Caprio – back in his better years – she sticks it up on the wall and slaps his cheek knowingly.* KATE *finds a very old packet of cigarettes and lights one – one drag and she realises it's ten years old, winces and carries on; another slug of wine.* KATE *pushes the bed around, the desk – rearranges furniture to try and recreate her childhood bedroom. In one corner of the room she gets hold of a corner of wallpaper and tries to pull it back – quite a big chuck of plaster comes off with it and she stops, a little alarmed.* KATE *pulls down another box, finds it full of old drawings and paintings – there is one of a family in a house, four windows and a front door, with Kate, Mum and Dad outside.* KATE *sticks it up on the wall. In the same box she pulls out a dress – it would fit a six-year-old perfectly; it's sweet – a light-pink pinafore dress, roses, white collar, not prissy.* KATE *smells it; she feels such fondness she can hardly bear it –* KATE *takes a small sip of wine –* KATE *takes off her top – staggering over to put her hand over Leonardo di Caprio's face/wag her finger at him whilst she does it.* KATE *puts on the dress – it's tiny – but she gets into it just about.* KATE *goes back to the box and finds an old projector – she plugs it in and sets it up to project against the back wall – she fiddles around with it for a moment – it flickers up a video – it's* KATE, *she's no older than ten – she's running around in the back garden with no clothes on doing cartwheels through the sprinkler, proud as punch and smiling furiously, she's having a ball, doing a little victory dance after each one.*

KATE *walks up to the wall and touches the face of her little self. She lies back against the wall and leans her face against the projection of her skin.* KATE *smiles;* KATE *seems overwhelmingly sad...*

ALBIN *enters.*

ALBIN. Kate – I've been for a walk and I've been thinking and I think –

KATE (*standing quickly*). No.

ALBIN *looks up at her – looks at the room.*

ALBIN. What are you doing?

KATE. I – please don't say.

ALBIN *notices the projection and stares – fondly.*

Pause.

ALBIN *looks back at the poster.*

ALBIN. Leo – really? He's such a prick.

KATE. Sorry. It was just – Romeo.

ALBIN. Oh.

KATE *rips down the poster.*

Silence.

KATE. State-dependent retrieval.

ALBIN. What?

KATE *lifts up the bottle.*

KATE. People can recall the information more accurately when intoxicated or –

ALBIN. If they've encoded the information in the same state.

KATE. Oh. Whoops.

ALBIN (*points at the projection*). You don't look pissed.

KATE. No.

Beat.

ALBIN. Kate, about earlier – about what I said earlier /

KATE. / I'm very confident.

ALBIN. Right, okay – but about –

KATE. I know it doesn't look like it – but I love my mum and
dad – and it was happy, it is /

ALBIN. / Can we just leave them out for a second, just listen –
I've been thinking about it, I've been walking for hours and
hours and I can't really feel my feet and I've been thinking
and – I don't think – I don't think /

KATE. / Shh – don't – I know, please – I – I know I've been,
shouting and doubt and breeds doubt, doubt breeds doubt – it
does – and – and – shouting breeds doubt and but I'm sorry
and I'm all fixed up now, no holes, look – no holes.

KATE *holds her arms open to him – 'Look, Mum, no holes' –
she's barely believing it.*

ALBIN *doesn't answer.*

Beat.

KATE *flounders a little.*

Well, just the one – (*Winks at* ALBIN.) eh?

KATE *points at her crotch – smirks.*

ALBIN. Okay – right – but – listen /

KATE. / No – wait – no, I have two holes – nearly forgot my
bum – but – but no holes in the middle – no holes in the –
middle – (*Lifts up the little dress and shows* ALBIN *that she
has no hole in the middle.*) see! Whole; whole like – with a
'W' – not – no holes.

ALBIN. That's great.

KATE. Weird that they're the same when they're opposite –
whole, hole, whole, hole.

ALBIN. Kate!

KATE. Please please please don't say it. (*Starting to cry.*)
Please. I'm trying – I'm really trying.

ALBIN. This is so selfish.

KATE. I know – I know it's horrible and selfish, yes – I know,
I'm sorry – it's repulsive – it's not –

ALBIN. Well, just stop it then.

KATE. I'm sorry – I'm really sorry.

ALBIN. Be stronger.

KATE (*bites her lip, stiffens up, nods her head.*) Yes. (*Gasps for
breath, tries to hold it in.*) Yes, yes.

ALBIN. Because this isn't love – it's need and that's so –
fucking – indiscriminate – do you understand, that's not… I
could be anyone – I could be anyone to fix this, just as long
as I'm here – and keep – fucking standing here – it's got
nothing to do with me – right now I could be anyone; do you
know how that feels?

KATE *nods, still trying to hold it together – nods, sorry –
silent, sorry.*

KATE. I'm sorry – I'm sorry –

ALBIN. Stop it – stop fucking saying that.

KATE *drags everything up in her to batten it all down – to
brave-face it, biting lip, choking it down.*

KATE. Yes.

Silence – some time – no one seems to be able to speak.

ALBIN *takes a step away from her.*

Al – I – when I was little – I have memories of when I was
little and I'm – I'm seeing through my eyes – do you know
what I mean? (*Closes her eyes.*) It's hot, it's summer and I'm
lying on my bed – my little single bed and my windows are
open and I can hear the fan going and feel breeze on me and
I'm naked, if I look at the memory I'm in my head I'm
looking at my body – I can see my little chest and toes and
the backs of my hands on the white sheets and I look up and
see the windows and I can hear the fan – I can hear it and I
feel the hot of my skin and the cool of the sheets, I can feel

myself pushing my little legs out to find a cold patch of sheet. Do you know what I /

ALBIN. / It's a field-perspective memory – you see the memory as if looking through your eyes at the time – you're *in* the memory – rather than observer memories where you watch yourself, you're detached and you stand outside the memory and watch it – like you watch a film. The field ones, where you're in it, are usually more emotional – more accurate.

KATE. All the other ones, I'm watching – I'm always watching, I'm never /

ALBIN. / Observer memories – necessarily inaccurate because you wouldn't have been watching yourself at the time.

KATE. All the ones from later – from – anywhere after about – eight or nine – I'm outside, I'm watching.

ALBIN. Usually the more recent memories are more sensory – and the earlier ones are observed – it's unusual for it to be the other way around.

KATE. I want to be back on that bed and naked because that – that memory is so different because it's just, it's just the heat of my skin and the cool of the sheets and the sound of the fan and there's nothing else – there's no – there's no noise in my head. (*Finding it hard.*) There's no fucking – questioning and worrying and fucking – standing outside and – and – commentating. I can't remember when that started but it isn't in that memory of the bed and I want to go back – so badly – because all the time, in all the others and worse and worse as I've got older – you pull out of everything – you're always – it's a wide-shot, it's a – do you know what I'm saying? It's never a close-up any more – I'm never in my eyes – I'm thinking instead, writing this second story – jotting it all down, there's no temperature or skin or sound – I remember – the – you know our first kiss; I can't remember how it feels, I just remember thinking – the sound of the thought of 'I wonder if I'm enjoying this – does this feel sparky, can I feel sparks here?' – that's what I fucking remember – not the feel, the touch – the – and sex – I'm seeing wallpaper, I'm thinking ceiling fans – not feeling –

ALBIN. Great, good to know – I'm so glad.

KATE. It's not you – it's not you, it's my fucking head; and sex – you then – sex – is the one time – still – most times – I'm back on that bed, there's silence and just – it shuts up a second – and I – when you're around I'm on holiday, for a minute.

Pause.

But all the rest of the time… I hate it. I want it to go away. I want to relax.

ALBIN. I don't like it much either.

KATE *sees the diaries on the floor, pages of writing lying around – she starts kicking them.*

KATE. Fucking diaries, fucking jotting it down – fucking nine years old I started this shit – thought it was smart or poetic or something, I wish someone had come and ripped the fucking pen out my hand and said go outside and run around, you self-interested pretentious little fucking idiot. /

ALBIN. / You were nine, Kate.

KATE. / You have no idea what you're doing to yourself – what you are setting up here – you fucking idiot. Put the fucking pen down! Why? Why did you start – why?

KATE *picks up a diary and throws it at the projection image.*

Pause.

ALBIN. Um –

KATE. I know. There's a hole, isn't there?

ALBIN Give it up.

KATE. Writing?

ALBIN. I don't want to spend my life with someone that's always watching.

Pause.

They look at one another.

KATE *shakes her head.*

I'm sorry –

KATE. I know.

ALBIN. I'm sorry – I'm really sorry – I'm sorry – I can't.

KATE. I know.

ALBIN *nods silently – yes – sorry – yes – biting it back – but yes, I'm sorry.*

KATE *takes a step towards* ALBIN.

ALBIN. You think it's a right – this special thing – that everyone should fucking respect – but what if it's not important? What if it's – actually just ego – just self-centred and destructive /

KATE. / I – it feels like I need to – if I don't I'll – get lost; really lost. On paper – there are – reasons for people being how they are – causes – there are good guys and bad guys and bad guys can learn and fix themselves – and –

ALBIN. But it doesn't have to be painful.

KATE. But it does have to be true.

ALBIN. They aren't the same thing.

Pause.

KATE *looks at* ALBIN.

What? You want to be Jayde – you think 'real gold' has to be trauma – and pain – and fuck everything that gets destroyed in the process? Hm? Bullshit. Bullshit does it. You're fine – you're a comfortable nice middle-class girl whose parents happened to divorce – well, big fucking deal, babe; it happens. And most people just get the fuck over it. They don't go rooting around trying to find the pain in every good fucking thing. You're fine – so grow up and stop spoiling everything – stop being so fucking self-indulgent!

Beat.

KATE. I started remembering in a house where… when I feel
loss and anger and hurt – it feels like the proper feeling, it
feels like the base note – the only real one actually and all
the others are just pretenders – and all that smiling and joy
and contentment are just fucking impostors and I know that
sounds ungrateful and spoilt and indulgent but those other
feelings can fuck right off because it's the pain that makes
you feel most alive – and that might be because I started my
being alive in a house that was filled with pain or it might
just be that pain and hurt and anger actually are the real
thing, the proper ones – the base notes – the closest we ever
really get to whatever it actually is to be alive. It's chicken-
and-egg maybe. But either way it feels like hard-wiring.

But since I met you – I've tried harder than I've ever fucking
tried – to believe bunnies and happy endings to pull myself
together and just get on with it – but, but you do have to
believe in it, you have to have faith in a thing, Al – it's not
just strapping a pair on and putting one foot in front of the
other – and I – I – I'd like to tell you – I'd like to make it
clear to you that believing – for me – believing things are
going to turn out okay – I mean for ever – I mean, to look at
the rest of it all and to see some kind of happy ending – I'd
like you to know – to be clear that that takes an almost
impossible – I mean – it feels like every single fucking cell is
sweating with the effort of looking at the horizon and trying
to see sun and my fists are tight and I'm trying as hard as
I've ever fucking tried for anything to see the blue sky and
the two-point-four and the happy-ever-after and I'm
squeezing the will, aching to generate because I *want* to –
because I *want* to believe so fucking badly – it's really all I
want – that's the thing – it's all I want – really – I just – I just
– there's this little Nazi inside of me that doesn't care about
anything but the wanting of that place – the wanting of that
place where it's safe and warm and there's the sun out and
the mama and the papa and the little babby and they all love
each other – and that little Nazi in there – it has big dreams
and the dreams make it feel nice – and it wants its world to
be safe and if that means that people have to die – if it means
they are cold because me and my three are warm then I don't
mind – my little Nazi doesn't mind as long as we three are

safe and warm. And so you do believe it – you believe in it
for a second – you see it like you're small and naked on a
bed – you see it like you're in it and there's no noise – and
then – and then – (*Beat.*) and then you're afraid – (*Beat.*) you
remember something else and you're afraid because it feels
like if you do believe it – then something bad is going to
happen – just come up and smack you in the face for being a
fucking idiot and not keeping your eyes out for the bad thing
– it'll smack you just for being stupid enough to not expect it
to jump up and smack you.

ALBIN. Shh. Stop – shh.

KATE *is gasping a bit – panicking.*

Shh.

ALBIN *takes the duvet off the bed and lays it on the floor –*
KATE *watches.*

ALBIN *makes* KATE *sit on the duvet.*

ALBIN *sits behind her and rocks her – like a little boat.*

I think it's just your brain, I think it's – okay.

KATE. What?

ALBIN. If you give a human half a loaf of bread – they're
happy. If you give the same human a whole loaf and take half
away – they're distressed; we're designed to feel the loss
more acutely. It's loss aversion – it's evolution, it's
economics – we're engineered not to let things be taken from
us. Your body tries to make you learn the lesson by replaying
the loss over and over again – in your head – if you think
through all the possible bad outcomes – if you go and find
the pain first – then you'll be prepared. If you can hurt
yourself before anyone else can, it won't be so bad if it
happens, you'll be ready.

KATE. Yeah.

ALBIN. It's just science. You're not crazy – it's not weak – it's
nature.

KATE. How do I change it?

ALBIN. A brain scan wouldn't be able to solve the flamingos.

KATE. Flamingos?

ALBIN. I was thinking – your mum remembers the notebook –
your dad remembers no notebook – the brain scans of the
recall of those two memory engrams would both show 'true'.

KATE. But they can't both be right.

ALBIN. Our brains can't tell the difference between something
that is actually true and something we believe to be true.

KATE. So?

ALBIN. There are some things that happened to you that you
never remember again – you just lose them – completely –
and the sad thing is that those things we lose are probably the
good bits – the humdrum frequent happy bits – the body
doesn't remember them because it doesn't need them for
anything. You can't remember what you had for breakfast
yesterday because you have breakfast every day and it's
pretty enjoyable and easy to do. You've just got to re-
remember. Get out all the good bits – go back, remember all
the good stuff – join all those dots – make that story instead.
Stop replaying the bad – stop being afraid that anyone is
going to go away. You don't need to protect yourself.

KATE. Don't I?

ALBIN. If we go wrong, it is going to hurt like fuck – and
thinking it through first, trying to defend yourself beforehand
– isn't going to make the blindest bit of fucking difference –
so you might as well not bother.

KATE *looks back at* ALBIN.

ALBIN *nods down at* KATE.

Beat.

Relax. Stop being afraid. Go back to being that little naked
kid on the bed – and just don't let the fear in – be brave and
relax. Tell your brain not to be afraid.

Silence – several seconds whilst the idea of it sits in KATE.

KATE. I'm very tired.

ALBIN. Me too.

KATE. Will you help me? I can't keep keeping the thingy in the cross hairs, keeping the – focusing on the – trying to –

ALBIN. Yes – I'll help you.

KATE. We'll lie down and close our eyes –

ALBIN. Yeah.

KATE. And we'll lie back and we'll just see – just see the dreams real and we'll build the pictures of it all and if we believe it then we can see it – and if we see it – together – with the living together and the baking and the cleaning and the shopping and the kids and the laughing and the getting old – if we can see it – if we can do that then we'll be okay – and all the worries, all the bad thoughts – we'll just blow them out – think them up and blow them out like whales – okay? Okay? Out our blowholes?

Both now lying on their backs like starfish . They both take in huge breaths and blow them out like whales – over and over again – big deep breaths in and then they blow them out like whales, blow them away.

Science is very good.

ALBIN. The best.

KATE climbs into ALBIN's arms and they curl around each other – they keep blowing.

KATE. I'd like to marry you if that's okay? If you'd – it looks rather nice.

ALBIN. Yes, please. That sounds lovely.

They keep blowing a little.

Can you turn 'naked you' off so we can sleep?

KATE. What?

ALBIN. The projector.

KATE. Oh – yes.

KATE *carefully unhooks herself from* ALBIN.

KATE *looks up at her little naked self once more – sort of says goodbye.*

KATE *goes to turn the projector off – she presses the wrong button and it clicks forward onto a new image – it's a holiday – no sound – eighties people moving around and talking, a dinner being had on a balcony – there's no one* KATE *recognises. Suddenly she stops the video – keeps it still – she's spotted something. In one corner – in the back of the picture –* KATE *walks towards the image –* IKE *and* NESSA *much younger, are holding hands and laughing – really laughing.*

KATE *puts her hand over the image of their hands.*

KATE *turns the projector off.*

LONDON

KATE *turns the printer on.*

KELSO

KATE *tucks herself back underneath* ALBIN.

KATE *turns the light off – they sleep.*

LONDON

The play prints.

KATE *lays down on the duvet – exhausted.*

KATE *sleeps.*

Nine

LONDON

KATE *sleeps on the duvet – alone.*

ALBIN *enters – sees* KATE *sleeping.*

ALBIN *goes to the printer and takes the script – he starts to read the play.*

The sun rises – it fills the office with light.

ALBIN *reads – time passes.*

ALBIN *sits, dressed in smart clothes, reading the printed script.*

ALBIN *finishes the script.*

KATE *rouses – confused.*

KATE. Oh.

> ALBIN *puts down the script.*
>
> *Pause.*

ALBIN. The science isn't bad. Not perfect but /

KATE. / Thanks.

> *Beat.*
>
> ALBIN *stands and starts to tidy the room.*

Do you mind?

ALBIN. You killed my parents.

KATE. It was just tidier – narrative-wise.

ALBIN. I'll let them know.

KATE. Al – I /

ALBIN. / Your parents, however, about to arrive – just rang, two minutes away – personally I can't wait, really excited –

sounds like I'm going to have a ball. Can't wait to meet your mum, bet she can't wait to meet me.

KATE. I'm sorry, I can change anything – I can /

ALBIN. / I haven't asked you to marry me.

Beat.

KATE. / I know.

ALBIN. I wasn't planning on – not any time soon, I –

KATE. I know.

ALBIN. This today – with your parents coming, you're not going to –

KATE. No – no – it's just – it was just –

ALBIN. Tidier?

KATE. Sort of.

ALBIN. Weird that it's in there before I've even…

KATE. I'm sorry.

The front-door buzzer goes.

They haven't been in the same room for twenty years, Al. It might be a bit –

ALBIN. You're still in your pyjamas.

KATE *starts desperately getting changed.*

KATE. I'll be ready. I'll sort everything – I just had to – It's done though, it's done.

Beat.

ALBIN. I'm pretty funny – I think I'm quite funny in there.

KATE. You're quite funny in real life.

ALBIN. Really?

KATE. Yeah.

ALBIN (*chuffed*). Hm.

The door buzzer goes again.

ALBIN *goes to the door.*

I'd never ask you to – you take what you get, all in.

KATE. I love you.

ALBIN *nods and exits to answer the door.*

KATE *stands and looks at the printed version of the play – holds it to her, it's done.*

KATE *places the play in a bottom drawer and shuts it – it's done.*

KATE *dresses quickly – smoothes down her hair.*

ALBIN *and* IKE *enter.*

IKE. Kate.

KATE. Hey, Dad.

IKE *hugs* KATE *– it's long – he means it – he's missed her.* KATE *hugs him back – with equal force.*

Dad – this is Albin.

IKE. We met at the door.

ALBIN. Can I take your coat?

IKE. I thought you'd be taller.

There's a knock at the door.

ALBIN. I'll get it.

IKE. Oh – lovely. He seems great.

KATE. He is.

Small beat – KATE *smiles.*

KATE *picks up a bowl on the side.*

Parmesan puff?

IKE. Don't mind if I do.

IKE *picks up the puff.*

ALBIN *enters.*

NESSA *enters*.

NESSA. Hello, Ike.

IKE. Nessa.

Beat.

ALBIN *takes* KATE*'s hand.*

Blackout.

End of play.

A Nick Hern Book

The Authorised Kate Bane first published in Great Britain as a paperback original in 2012 by Nick Hern Books Limited, The Glasshouse, 49a Goldhawk Road, London W12 8QP, in association with Grid Iron Theatre Company

Cover photo by Douglas Jones; title design by Emma Quinn
Cover design by Ned Hoste, 2H

Typeset by Nick Hern Books, London
Printed in the UK by 4Edge, Essex

A CIP catalogue record for this book is available from the British Library

ISBN   978 1 84842 309 1